The Weight of Nightmares

The Weight of Nightmares

Time and the Politics of Reparations for Slavery

Kenan Van de Mieroop-Al Bahrani

VERSO
London • New York

First published by Verso 2026

The manufacturer's authorized representative in the EU for product safety (GPSR) is LOGOS EUROPE, 9 rue Nicolas Poussin, 17000, La Rochelle, France
contact@logoseurope.eu

1 3 5 7 9 10 8 6 4 2

Verso
UK: 6 Meard Street, London W1F 0EG
US: 207 East 32nd Street, New York, NY 10016
versobooks.com

Verso is the imprint of New Left Books

ISBN-13: 978-1-83674-168-8
ISBN-13: 978-1-83674-169-5 (UK EBK)
ISBN-13: 978-1-83674-170-1 (US EBK)

British Library Cataloguing in Publication Data
A catalogue record for this book is available from the British Library

Library of Congress Cataloging-in-Publication Data
A catalog record for this book is available from the Library of Congress

Typeset in Minion by Hewer Text UK Ltd, Edinburgh
Printed and bound by CPI Group (UK) Ltd, Croydon CR0 4YY

Humans fear time, but time fears the pyramids

Arabic proverb, *The Oxford Dictionary of Proverbs*

Contents

Acknowledgments

This manuscript was composed over a two-year period between the late winter of 2021 and the spring of 2023, but the questions that motivated me to write the book have been on my mind for as long as I can remember. During that time, I benefited from the help and encouragement of people too numerous to mention here. So, this message of acknowledgment is incomplete.

Nevertheless, I would like to thank everyone at Verso and, in particular, Sebastian Budgen for their contributions to this project.

I would also like to thank some of those who read and discussed parts of this book and helped me to sharpen the ideas within it. In particular, the inspiration and continued mentorship of Berber Bevernage have been essential. My old colleagues and friends at Ghent University in both the INTH and the Tapas group provided a venue to test out my arguments at an early stage. Those groups remain two of the most dynamic and stimulating intellectual settings I know of anywhere in the world. Kalle Pihlainen and the participants in the Philosophy of History Seminar series at the Institute of Historical Research in London allowed me to share the work that would eventually transform into the second chapter of this book and provided wonderful feedback. At Leiden University, I wish to acknowledge the PCNI group and Herman Paul for reading the third chapter. I also want to express my appreciation to the students in my course, A Cultural History of Time. I am also very grateful to Pepijn Brandon for taking the time to discuss some of the issues I address in fourth chapter with me.

Outside these institutions, several close friends and family have helped me along the way. Thank you to Houssine and Jaafar for countless stimulating conversations. I am also extremely grateful to Hilde, Rik, and Andrea. I want to extend a special thanks to Mona Al Khalidi.

A great deal of this book deals with intergenerational relations. It is impossible to express the profound debt I owe to my parents for their love and guidance, which has taken so many different forms over many years. Their support has been not only crucial to the completion of this book but also sustaining during the most difficult periods.

I am extraordinarily lucky to have been able to enjoy Maud's daily and hourly love and encouragement. She was vital to every step of this project and the prime motivator helping me to push through to its completion. I could never have done it without her. Arda also did his part by bringing joy to me every day, and he continues to make me proud.

I dedicate this book the memory of my son Hector. With all my love.

1

Temporal Power

Racial time is defined as the inequalities of temporality that result from power relations between racially dominant and subordinate groups.
—Michael Hanchard, "Afro-Modernity: Temporality, Politics, and the African Diaspora"

It is a view that abjures history's redemptive function, instead taking history to be a record of discontinuity and multiple temporalities (the lived times of the enslaved and their descendants are different from those of white Americans), a process of contention and conflict, a story of struggles with and for power, with no sharp boundaries between past, present, and future.
—Joan Wallach Scott, *On the Judgment of History*

The time has come to call upon each to realize his own destiny. The progress of human Reason laid the basis for this great Revolution and you shall now assume the particular duty of hastening its pace.
—Maximilien Robespierre, in Reinhart Koselleck, *Futures Past*

One of the many peculiar things about the controversy surrounding reparations for slavery and colonialism is that it has generated so much discussion about temporality. In courtrooms, the time bar or statute of limitations has regularly been invoked to dismiss claims. Critics usually say that slavery and colonialism are things of the past and took place too long ago for anything to be done about them now. In any case, they argue, it is wrong to hold people living today accountable for the sins of their ancestors. For some, reparations movements are harbingers of a postmodern and retrospective form of politics—a politics of the past, or of repentance—that signals the abandonment of the future-oriented and utopian visions that characterized modernity. For others, reparations claims are nothing less than an attack on "our civilization" and the fact that they are even being considered is evidence of the historic decline of the "West" and a form of cultural "suicide."[1]

But "the past is never dead. It's not even past." William Faulkner's famous phrase is sometimes quoted by those wishing to put across the view that the legacies of slavery and colonialism persist into the present. These legacies are both "symbolic" and "material"; through memory, cultural trauma, and structures—social, economic, and political—the past continues to shape the world today. In legal terms, these continuing violations and compounding injustices mean that the statute of limitations must be equitably tolled; the legal clock must be stopped. Crimes against humanity are, in any case, imprescriptible. Political philosophers have sought to articulate theories of intergenerational justice that would support an idea of reparations. Advocates of reparations, meanwhile, regularly speak of them in utopian terms as a "racial reckoning," or moments of justice in the future. This moment may be conceived as the fulfilment of the prefigured promise of a more inclusive society. But, often, reparations are understood as a means that can be used to achieve a different end: the foundation of a new society.

All these wide-ranging arguments are rooted, to some extent, in ideas—whether explicitly stated or only implicit—about the ways in which groups and individuals relate to time, or how they ought to. They point to something about the reparations debates that has often been noted but rarely elaborated in any detail—namely, that they reveal a politics of time.

1 Éric Zemmour, *Le suicide français* (Paris: Albin Michel, 2014).

A politics of time

Time can be a subject of political struggle that is every bit as contentious as the organization and distribution of space. But, whereas designations of space are usually understood to be historical artifacts and the product of, usually violent, conflict, the distribution of time is often spoken of or regarded as if it were natural. To be sure, geographical divisions are also habitually dressed up in the language of nature, a divine or cosmic destiny, yet it is widely understood that humans drew the lines that divide the world. It is less obvious that divisions of time are also amenable to manipulation. There are clear limits to humanity's power over time; at least, if what we mean by "time" is what physicists mean when they discuss it as a parameter, or as space-time. Time, in that sense, cannot be manipulated in a socially or politically meaningful way. We cannot turn it back, we cannot travel in it, and we certainly cannot make more of it. The empirical observation that time moves more slowly at sea level than at the top of a mountain makes no difference to the way people live their lives. But, insofar as we are talking about time as a significant aspect of the symbolic world of human thought and action, time is configured and distributed. There can be multiple configurations and distributions of time which serve different ends, and these are always open and vulnerable to being further reconfigured and redistributed. It is precisely for this reason that one may speak of a politics of time, or of political struggle over the designation and enforcement of a particular temporality.

The significance of temporality was fully understood at what is often said to be the founding moment of modern politics: the French Revolution. In 1793, a new Republican calendar was introduced, retroactively declaring the previous year the first of a new era. The calendar, which was in use for almost thirteen years, was more than a symbolic gesture. In her detailed historical study, Sanja Perovic explains that the calendar was thought necessary precisely because it was understood that conceptions of time were a central source of legitimacy in the *ancien régime*. As she explains, "the Christian calendar subtended a vertical hierarchy consisting of three distinct social classes (those who toiled, those who prayed and those who fought)."[2] Before the

2 Sanja Perovic, *The Calendar in Revolutionary France: Perceptions of Time in Literature, Culture, Politics* (Cambridge: Cambridge University Press, 2015), 37.

revolution, almanacs and calendars synchronized sublunary affairs and inscribed agricultural activities, loan repayments, feast days, and dynasties in a Christian cosmology and story of salvation.[3] Political institutions and the tasks of everyday life were coordinated and imbued with a broader significance and backed by what was thought of as a divine plan. Founding a new society based upon new ideals, therefore, required nothing less than overturning the temporality of the old regime. "For Gilbert Romme, the [Republican] calendar's chief architect, the calendar marked the epoch when the history of the French Revolution converged with nature itself, when natural equality and the power of human beings over their own history became one and the same."[4]

This episode reveals at least two important things about what I call the politics of time. First, the revolutionaries grasped a point, which one also finds in self-help books on time management that decorate the bookshelves at train stations and airports around the world today: In order to find true freedom, people must take charge of their own schedules. But this is much easier said than done, especially when confronted—as the French revolutionaries certainly were—with powerful forces of reaction.

Second, one of the most common tactics within the politics of time is to elide the difference between time and temporality. Powerful actors attempt to reify particular configurations and distributions of human time and present them as a matter of metaphysical principle. This kind of reification has the effect of limiting the scope of the politics of time and legitimizing a given order. The French Revolution thus replaced a temporality rooted in appeals to godly authority with one that was said to draw its mandate from nature itself.

But, as the example of the revolutionary calendar shows clearly, temporality is not fixed; it takes on different forms across times and cultures. Different cultures of time have been a significant subject of investigation in the field of anthropology, and the cultural history of time has become the subject of renewed interest within the discipline of history. European encounters with other cultures and their calendars animated a debate about the link between social orders and time in the

3 Perovic notes the semantic connection between the word "calendar" and the Latin word *calendarium*, which means "accounting book." Ibid., 24.

4 Ibid., 1.

eighteenth century, and these discussions formed the background against which the Republican calendar was conceived.[5] In the twentieth century, E. E. Evans-Pritchard and Claude Lévi-Strauss showed the connection between patterns of economic and social life and concepts of time and history.[6] Albeit in a very different way to the French revolutionaries, the Nuer also used categories of time that connected and coordinated their social and economic activities with the demands of their environment. Their terms, *Tot* and *Mei*, denoted at once the dry and wet seasons of the year as well as the type of activities (agriculture, fishing, herding) to be undertaken during these periods. The time of day was noted by referring to habitual practices, so that one might say, "I will return at (the time of) milking."[7] These kinds of observations seemed to confirm Émile Durkheim's insight that it was "the rhythm of social life which is at the basis of the category of time."[8]

The fascination with exotic temporalities in the earlier part of the twentieth century was also motivated by an interest in how "social activities and structures" in Europe produced particular "time-values."[9] Discourses about how other cultures relate to time became part of a broader constellation of ideas about the "modern West." The idea that "the West" has had its own new and unique temporality in the form of "modernity," and subsequently of "postmodernity," is one of the most widely repeated and discussed propositions in the humanities. Most of the scholarly literature on cultures of time deals, in one way or another, with the vexed question of modernity. And one of the many contentious points in those discussions has been the historiographical problem of determining when exactly this new relationship to time emerged.

That debate has been shaped most significantly by the German conceptual historian Reinhart Koselleck.[10] His argument that a

5 Ibid., 26–33.

6 E. E. Evans-Pritchard, "Nuer Time-Reckoning," *Africa: Journal of the International African Institute* 12, no. 2 (1939): 189–216. Also see Alfred Gell, *The Anthropology of Time: Cultural Constructions of Temporal Maps and Images* (Oxford: Berg, 1992).

7 Evans-Pritchard, "Nuer Time-Reckoning," 207.

8 Émile Durkheim, *The Elementary Forms of Religious Life*, trans. Joseph Ward Swain (London: George Allen & Unwin, 1915), Project Gutenberg, November 13, 2012, 440.

9 Evans-Pritchard "Nuer Time-Reckoning," 189.

10 On this question, see also Zachary S. Schiffman, *The Birth of the Past* (Baltimore: Johns Hopkins University Press, 2011).

transformative period of European history—*Sattelzeit*—produced a qualitatively new, and generalized, experience of time—*Neuzeit*—continues to enjoy widespread appreciation even in light of the serious criticisms to which it has been subjected.[11] Before *Sattelzeit*, Christians understood the events of the world as being governed by an already fixed plan as outlined in the story of Creation, Incarnation, Christ's Second Coming, and the Last Judgment. The future, meanwhile, was expected to be much like the past, and political events were seen as similar in kind, or parallel to events of the historical past. The idea that nothing fundamentally new ever happened was captured in the phrase from Ecclesiastes *nihil sub sole novum,* there is nothing new under the sun.[12] But this picture was undermined over the course of three centuries following the Reformation during which the End of the World was continually "prorogued."[13] Political revolutions, social and economic upheaval, and technological changes led people to begin to expect that the next generations would experience a fundamentally different world to the one their ancestors had lived in, or the one that they had known before. These factors combined to produce a split between the "space of experience" and the "horizon of expectation"—two metahistorical categories. If Robespierre could declare that the meaning of history is Progress and exhort his co-revolutionaries to hasten the pace of its coming, it was only because a previously dominant idea of time and history governed by providential design had already eroded.

François Hartog has elaborated upon this account of the history of time consciousness and extended it to the current era. He identifies three distinct regimes of historicity in "Western" culture.[14] In the

11 Kathleen Davis, *Periodization and Sovereignty: How Ideas of Feudalism and Secularization Govern the Politics of Time* (Philadelphia: University of Pennsylvania Press, 2012); Judith Pollmann, *Memory in Early Modern Europe, 1500–1800* (Oxford: Oxford University Press, 2017), especially the chapter "Past and Present: The Virtues of Anachronism."

12 Reinhart Koselleck, *Futures Past*, trans. Keith Tribe (New York: Columbia University Press, 2004), 133.

13 Ibid., 22.

14 He defines his key term as follows: "I defined 'regime of historicity' in two ways: in a restricted sense, as the way in which a given society approaches its past and reflects upon it; and in a broader sense, as 'the modalities of self-consciousness that each and every society adopts in its constructions of time and its perceptions. To borrow Lévi-Strauss's terms . . . the notion refers to how a particular human community 'reacts' to a 'degree of historicity' which is the same in all societies. More specifically, it is a tool for

first—the so-called *ancien* or Christian regime of historicity—the space of experience seemed to coincide with the horizon of expectation, and the past was valorized as a source of authority and a repository of examples that could guide decisions in the present. The phrase *historia magistrate vitae*, "history as life's teacher," reflected an understating that knowledge of the past had a practical function. But the French Revolution gave birth to a new and modern regime of historicity in which—as Koselleck had already argued—this *topos* no longer seemed persuasive since the future was now expected to be substantially different from the past. Modernity was marked precisely by the belief in the possibility of making new futures and utopian visions of progress. Europe—at least certain parts of it—was said to be at the vanguard of history with a capital *H*, now understood as a collective singular process.[15] The future, not the past, became the new source of authority and legitimacy. Changes in the perception and "experience" of time were occasioned by upheavals in politics, society, and economy that had taken place during the foregoing century and were reflected in a culture fascinated by new technologies and the phenomenon of time itself.

But as changes continued apace, cracks began to emerge in the futurist regime as well. The dramatic events of the twentieth century expanded the gap between the space of experience and the horizon of expectation into a chasm so large that the future faded from view. It now appears—to Hartog at least—that "we" are living in a continuous present; an omnipresent present saturated by a sense of confusion and disorientation. Under this presentist regime of historicity, acceleration has become so intense that it has generated a veritable crisis of time.

One of the "symptoms" of this temporal "malaise" is—Pierre Nora tells us—the widespread turn to "memory." Desperate to find some sort of firm ground to hold on to amid the slippage, many have sought to cling to their collective memories. Now that all grand narratives have

comparing different types of history, and also (or above all, I would now say) for highlighting modes of relation to time, and exploring forms of temporal experience here and elsewhere, today and in the past—in short, it serves to explore ways of being in time." François Hartog, *Regimes of Historicity: Presentism and Experiences of Time*, trans. S. Brown (New York: Columbia University Press, 2015), 9.

15 The idea that history should be understood as a "collective singular" process, replacing the notion of disparate histories, occurred during the same period according to Koselleck, *Futures Past*, 36.

apparently been abandoned, people have turned their political interests to the past instead of attempting to project their hopes onto an uncertain future. Some insist that calls for reparations for slavery must be viewed within this context.[16]

Hartog's account—along with much of the scholarship on modernity and postmodernity which it resembles—shares something in common with a great deal of self-help and time-management literature. Such texts emphatically state that the perception and the reality that things are changing ever more quickly is the most important phenomenon in the world today. And they quite rightly note that this can be a source of great anxiety. But the explanations remain vague as to why these changes are occurring. There is a tendency to speak as though time is speeding up or accelerating of its own accord. When a cause for the rapid pace of change is mentioned, it is usually identified as "technology," while, in the writings of Hartog and Koselleck, it is explained as a combination of new technologies and rapid political and social changes. But, surely, these changes are themselves as much the result of the acceleration as they are its cause.

If the acceleration of (post)modernity is a sort of mysterious force or historical epoch that organically unfolded, there is nothing much that can be done about it. One can only resign oneself to it and hew to the imperatives of the changing times. But it is obviously not time itself that is speeding up, as Christophe Bouton notes: "Acceleration which is in its origin a central concept of Newtonian physics, is measured by time; it designates the augmentation of speed with respect to time. Therefore, time itself cannot accelerate because it would require another time in order to measure such an acceleration."[17] So—to reformulate the question—if the acceleration is really one of the pace and intensity of human affairs, what explains it?

It is hardly a coincidence that almost all the accounts that actually offer an explanation for this phenomenon are rooted in Marxian

16 I elaborate and subject such accounts to critique in greater detail in chapter 5 of this book. There I show that the idea of reparations for slavery is presented as another symptom of the same phenomenon in this discourse. I have also discussed this point more extensively in Kenan Van de Mieroop, "The 'Age of Commemoration' as a Narrative Construct: A Critique of the Discourse on the Contemporary Crisis of Memory in France," *Rethinking History* 22, no. 2 (2016): 172–91.

17 Christophe Bouton, *L'Accélération de l'histoire: Des Lumières à l'Anthropocène* (Paris: Seuil, 2022), 13 (my translation).

economic theory. This is not, as right-wing pundits would have us believe, because academia has been overrun by Marxists. It is, rather, a reflection of the fact that—in contrast to neoclassical economics which understands technology to be an exogenous factor in economic growth—the Marxian framework coherently explains why capitalism is so technologically dynamic and disruptive.[18] The coercive forces of competition drive capital to find new ways to augment the production of surplus value and profit. Technological change in the realms of production, circulation, and consumption provides a competitive edge. This understanding underlies Fredric Jameson's account of postmodernism as a cultural dominant that is connected to what he calls (following Ernest Mandel) late capitalism.[19] If, as David Harvey notes, there has been space-time compression, it is because changes in the production process and communication technologies have facilitated new modes of flexible accumulation.[20] Hartmut Rosa gives the most detailed explanation of the phenomenon of "social acceleration," and identifies three "motors" that drive the process: These are cultural, sociocultural, and economic in nature. In the end, the drive to produce value in capitalism is the decisive factor.[21] Changes in the lived experiences of time at a given moment in European history had much to do with the subsumption of ever greater parts of the world into a new mode of production and distribution.

For many, if not most people, the "emergence" of the (post)modern experience of time might more accurately be described as an imposition. Moreover, declarations about the modern era were not merely descriptions of an observed reality, they were also performative

18 There are also endogenous theories of growth—for instance, the one associated with Paul Michael Romer.

19 Fredric Jameson, "Postmodernism, or the Cultural Logic of Late Capitalism," *New Left Review* 1, no. 146 (July–August 1984): 53–92.

20 David Harvey, *The Condition of Postmodernity: An Enquiry into the Origins of Cultural Change* (Cambridge, MA: Blackwell, 1990). See especially chapter 17.

21 Hartmut Rosa, *Social Acceleration: A New Theory of Modernity*, trans. Jonathan Trejo-Mathys (New York: Columbia University Press, 2013), 162, 194. See also Barbara Adam, "When Time Is Money: Contested Rationalities of Time in the Theory and Practice of Work," *Theoria: A Journal of Social and Political Theory* 102 (2003): 94–125. Bouton, who prefers to speak about the "acceleration of history," also emphasizes the importance of Marxian accounts of technological development. Bouton, *L'Accélération de l'histoire*, 37–8.

statements. That is because modernity was always more than simply a chronological concept. Rather the "qualitatively new" temporality of modernity involved the active "valorization of the historical (as opposed to the merely chronological) present over the past, as its negation and transcendence, and as the standpoint from which to periodize and understand history as a whole." These words of Peter Osborne reflect the view that modernity has a triple status as at once a declaration, a demand, and a command to "be modern."[22] Looked at in this way, a new question emerges which is more manifestly a political one: Who has articulated the injunction to be modern and why?

Is not modernity really what Paul Gilroy calls the time of Paris, Berlin, and London?[23] The phrase reminds us that the temporality of the metropoles was spread throughout the world by the rhythms of capitalist accumulation and imperial expansion. It was conveyed by trade, armies, and technologies, and it was given legal force by states. The time zones that divide the globe were instituted first by railroad companies before they were adopted in the International Meridian Conference of 1884. Time discipline was inculcated in the multitudes laboring in the factory and on the plantation.[24] Alongside these processes, new forms of historical consciousness were promoted by nationalist ideologies and notions of citizenship.[25] Modern academic historiography was, at its inception, deeply bound up in projects of nation-building and took the geographical boundaries of nation-states as its implicit spatial framework. Meanwhile, "the modern 'academic' conception of time," Chris Lorenz explains, "is a secularized version of the rectilinear, irreversible Christian time conception, stripped of its

22 Peter Osborne, "Modernity Is a Qualitative, Not a Chronological, Category," *New Left Review* 1, no. 192 (1992): 73; and Peter Osborne, "Global Modernity and the Contemporary: Two Categories of the Philosophy of Historical Time," in Chris Lorenz and Berber Bevernage, eds., *Breaking Up Time: Negotiating the Borders Between Past and Present* (Göttingen: Vandenhoeck & Ruprecht, 2013), 71.

23 Paul Gilroy, *The Black Atlantic: Modernity and Double Consciousness* (London: Verso, 1993), 197.

24 E. P. Thompson, "Time, Work-Discipline, and Industrial Capitalism," *Past and Present* 38 (1967): 56–97; Mark Michael Smith, *Mastered by the Clock: Time, Slavery, and Freedom in the American South* (Chapel Hill: University of North Carolina Press, 1997).

25 Stefan Berger and Christoph Conrad, *The Past as History: National Identity and Historical Consciousness in Modern Europe* (London: Palgrave, 2015); Stefan Berger and Chris Lorenz, eds., *Nationalizing the Past: Historians as Nation Builders in Modern Europe* (London: Palgrave, 2010).

notion of an end and reduced to the idea of a structured process."[26] There is, therefore, a sense in which the command to be modern has always meant conforming to what is expected of the citizen of a capitalist nation-state. It has also meant that millions have been placed outside its geographical-temporal purview.

Understood as a category of time, (post)modernity must be a totalizing and universal experience. Understood as a description of a temporality, however, it is easier to see that the speed up and acceleration have not affected everyone in the same way.[27] This is well documented empirically. Judy Wajcman explains that experiences of time stress vary across groups and individuals, and that gender, class, and ethnicity play no small role.[28] She recounts, for example, that studies reveal a "polarization of working time between those who work very long hours and others who work few or no hours . . . The fifty-plus hours week is . . . predominantly a characteristic of the professional and managerial class."[29] While dual-earner households, where both partners work full time, have become predominant in certain countries, domestic work and care still fall overwhelmingly on the shoulders of women. "Indeed, time-use data suggests that time poverty is a particularly widespread experience among working mothers, who juggle work, family and leisure."[30] At the other end of the temporal spectrum, waiting and the overabundance of time pervade the lives of the unemployed and individuals pushed to the margins of processes of accumulation.[31] It is

26 Chris Lorenz, "Unstuck in Time: The Sudden Presence of the Past," in Karin Tilmans, Frank van Vree, and Jay Winter, eds., *Performing the Past: Memory, History, and Identity in Modern Europe* (Amsterdam: Amsterdam University Press, 77).

27 Jameson's phrase "cultural dominant" leaves space for this. Hartmut Rosa, meanwhile, insists that in analyzing social acceleration, he does not deny the diversity of temporal experiences, but nevertheless wants to focus on what he believes to be a powerful and central dynamic.

28 Judy Wajcman, *Pressed for Time: The Acceleration of Life in Digital Capitalism* (Chicago: University of Chicago Press, 2015), 34. Furthermore, scholarship in disability studies has highlighted assumptions underpinning notions of temporality through the concept of "crip time." Ellen Samuels, "Six Ways of Looking at Crip Time," *Disability Studies Quarterly* 37, no. 3 (Summer 2017).

29 Ibid., 65.

30 Wajcman, *Pressed for Time*, 66.

31 A key issue in recent anthropological studies of time and inequality has been waiting. See, for example, June Hee Kwon, "The Work of Waiting: Love and Money in Korean Chinese Transnational Migration," *Cultural Anthropology* 30, no. 3 (2015):

not hard to imagine that the billions of people in the global reserve army of labor are likely to have very different relationships to this temporal scheme.

If the lived time of individuals is diverse, the historical consciousness of modernity is, as postcolonial critics have already pointed out, also far from universal. Indeed, that may have been the point all along. Because, as Edward Said has argued, the construction of the identity of the "modern West" was facilitated by the articulation of that region's fundamental difference and uniqueness vis-à-vis the rest of the world; a process that involved the designation of the non-West as the inferior and deficient opposite on multiple levels. One of those levels is that of time itself. The rest of the world was spoken and written about as non-modern, backward, decadent, or, as Hegel said of Africa, remaining in a timeless state outside history altogether. This temporal scheme provided a crucial justification for colonialism.

Claims to modernity were used to distinguish and separate certain groups from their contemporaries. Johannes Fabian famously argued that the discipline of anthropology as a whole was engaged in a practice of "allochronic" distancing of its subject, denying their "coevalness" with the "modern West."[32] At the same time, Dipesh Chakrabarty claims, the "historicity" of the "West" remains the standard against which the history of all regions is measured.[33] This is even more clear in the discipline of economics, where belief in historical progress is alive and well, so that it is a matter of etiquette today to speak of "developing" and developed countries. The political implications of this terminology are that the rest of the world is behind the times and needs to play a game of catch-up in order to follow the West down the path it has forged.[34] The

477–500; Craig Jeffry, *Timepass: Youth, Class, and the Politics of Waiting in India* (Stanford, CA: Stanford University Press, 2010); Javier Auyero, *Patients of the State: The Politics of Waiting in Argentina* (Durham, NC: Duke University Press, 2012); Daniel Mains, "Neoliberal Times: Progress, Boredom, and Shame Among Young Men in Urban Ethiopia," *American Ethnologist* 34, no. 4 (2007): 659–73.

32 Johannes Fabian, *Time and the Other: How Anthropology Makes Its Object* (New York: Columbia University Press, 2014 [1983]).

33 Dipesh Chakrabarty, *Provincializing Europe: Postcolonial Thought and Historical Difference* (Princeton, NJ: Princeton University Press, 2008).

34 I follow the argument made by Said and many others that the idea of a homogeneous and coherent "West" is a problematic concept for reasons too numerous to explain in a footnote. That is why I have thus far spoken about the so-called West or put the

policy prescriptions of so-called development organizations based in Washington, DC, and other "Western" capitals are thereby endowed with an aura of historical destiny.

Meanwhile the notion that there is anything like *the* space of experience, in the singular, appears absurd in the light of the volumes of scholarship on "collective memory" which have documented the incredibly diverse mnemonic practices that proliferated in the past and continue today. Much of that literature had been devoted to explaining how the memory of slavery has been alternatively repressed, forgotten, or recalled and passed down, through commemorative practices and "cultural trauma."[35] Even within the geographical boundaries of the so-called West, modernity has always had its countercultures. Time was a central preoccupation among thinkers in the "Black Atlantic" who, to quote the inimitable Gilroy once again, "repudiated the heroic narrative of western civilization and used a philosophically informed approach to slavery in order to undermine the monumental time that supports it."[36] W. E. B. Du Bois's notion of "double consciousness," Alain Locke's exposition of the "New Negro," the poetry of Langston Hughes, the paintings of Aaron Douglas, Ralph Ellison's concept of "invisibility"—in which

word in quotation marks. To make the text more readable, however, I have chosen to use the term without quotation marks throughout the rest of the book.

35 This is a very large body of literature. Some notable works include: James Oliver Horton, *Slavery and Public History: The Tough Stuff of American Memory* (New York: New Press, 2006); Michel-Rolph Trouillot, *Silencing the Past: Power and the Production of History* (Boston: Beacon Press, 2015); Myriam Cottias, "L'oubli du passé contre la citoyenneté: troc et ressentiment à la Martinique (1848–1946)," in Fred Constant and Justin Daniel, eds., *1946–1996: Cinquante ans de départementalisation outre-mer* (Paris: L'Harmattan, 1997); Françoise Vèrges, *La Mémoire enchainée: Questions sur l'esclavage* (Paris: Albin Michel, 2006); Elizabeth Kowaleski Wallace, *The British Slave Trade and Public Memory* (New York: Columbia University Press, 2006); Ana Lucia Araujo, *Public Memory of Slavery* (Amherst, NY: Cambria Press, 2010); Gloria Wekker, *White Innocence: Paradoxes of Colonialism and Race* (Durham, NC: Duke University Press, 2016); Esther Captain, "The Selective Forgetting and Remodeling of the Past: Postcolonial Legacies in the Netherlands," in Stefan Jonsson and Julia Willén, eds., *Austere Histories in European Societies* (London: Routledge, 2016), 73–87; Herman Ogoti Kiriama, *The Legacy of Slavery in Coastal Kenya: Memory, Identity, and Heritage* (Lanham, MD: Rowman & Littlefield, 2022); Ron Eyerman, *Cultural Trauma: Slavery and the Formation of African American Identity* (Cambridge: Cambridge University Press, 2001). For a very important critique of the discourse on trauma see Wulf Kansteiner, "Genealogy of a Category Mistake: A Critical Intellectual History of the Cultural Trauma Metaphor," *Rethinking History* 8, no. 2 (2004), 193–221.

36 Gilroy, *Black Atlantic*, 197.

one has a "different sense of time, you're never quite on the beat"—and the Afrocentrism of Molefi Kete Asante, in which European modernity is re-narrated as an interlude in a broader history between an ancient African past and an Afrocentric future; all dealt with the problem of temporality. Sun Ra's 1974 film *Space Is the Place* is a powerful and insightful commentary on the dominant politics of time. Sun Ra is not born in time, he "arrives" in order to lift the youth of Oakland into a new historicity whose telos is an Afrofuturist utopia.

From a politics to a poetics of time

So, even if the temporality of capital accumulation and the historicity of modern nation-states have been prominent, they have always existed alongside multiple other temporal strategies—that is to say, alongside different ways of configuring and distributing time.[37] Temporalities can come into conflict with one another, and when they do, we can speak of a politics of time, or what Charles Mills calls a chronopolitics.[38]

37 The idea of multiple temporalities is now an important issue in the field of the theory and philosophy of history. See my article with Berber Bevernage, Broos Delanote, Anton Froeyman, Patty Huijbers, and Gisele Iecker de Almeida, "Philosophy of History After 1945: A Bibliometric Study," *History and Theory* 58, no. 3 (2019): 406–36. Also see Helge Jordheim, "Against Periodization: Koselleck's Theory of Multiple Temporalities," *History and Theory* 51, no. 2 (2012): 151–71. The observation that there are multiple temporalities that sometimes exist in a conflictual relationship was central to the volume by Dan Edelstein, Stefanos Geroulanos, and Natasha Wheatley, eds., *Power and Time: Temporalities in Conflict and the Making of History* (Chicago: University of Chicago Press, 2020).

38 Charles W. Mills, "The Chronopolitics of Racial Time," *Time and Society* 29, no. 2 (2020): 297–317. Among the most significant recent works on the politics of time are those of Berber Bevernage and Sarah Sharma. Bevernage shows, for example, that a politics of time is at play in processes of transitional justice when new political regimes appeal to the "time of history" in order to bury the past they see as problematic and move on, while victims and survivors call upon the "time of justice" to seek redress for past misdeeds, a distinction he takes from Henry Russo. The contradiction between these two times is rooted in their different views of the reversibility of time: The "discourse of jurisdiction assumes a reversible time in which the crime is, as it were, still wholly present and able to be reversed, annulled or compensated by the correct sentence or punishment." But "modern historical discourse"—in which the arrow of time is irreversible—is deployed by authorities to close off the problematic past and urge the political community to move on. Berber Bevernage, *History, Memory, and State-Sponsored Violence: Time and Justice* (London: Routledge, 2012), 2, 11. Meanwhile

The debates about reparations for slavery and colonialism exemplify one such political conflict over temporality. By tracing the different and antithetical ways in which conceptions of temporality come into play within the reparations debates, this book aims to clarify and explain how the management and categorization of time have political implications and reflect relations of power. It takes a descriptive and critical rather than a normative approach to the study of the politics of time. In this book I will not attempt to follow the path outlined by Hartmut Rosa and provide a "social-scientific diagnosis of *the times* (*Zeitdiagnose*)."[39] On the contrary, I want to portray temporality as a site of perpetual struggle. Nor do I intend to suggest—as some literature on the topic of reparations sometimes casually does—that different groups and individuals are living in different times. The point is, rather, to show that the politics of time involves the implementation of time-management strategies and the invocation of different temporal instruments to achieve specific ends. In the case of the reparations debates, these instruments are not drawn from different cultural registers. The strategies deployed in the debate about reparations for slavery are not foreign imports or even recent innovations to be dismissed as "woke"; they are all well established in the traditions of the modern West.

My arguments are rooted in an understanding that temporality—in its social and phenomenological dimensions—is not a neutral category or parameter; it is a narrative configuration that coordinates the rhythms of social life. This position on narrative temporality is close to that advanced by Paul Ricoeur, and the present volume maintains a constructively critical relation to his work.[40] In assigning narrative a transcendental role, Ricoeur offered a *poetic*, rather than a logical solution to what he described as the aporias that have plagued the philosophy of time throughout history. Time is subject to a *poiesis* when it is configured through narration into a

Sharma uses the term "power-chronography" to describe the conflicting temporalities of interpersonal relations she has observed in urban settings: Sarah Sharma, *In the Meantime: Temporality and Cultural Politics* (Durham, NC: Duke University Press, 2014). Also see Tanya Ann Kennedy, "From Combahee Resistance to the Confederate: Black Feminist Temporalities and White Supremacy," *Time and Society* 29, no. 2 (2020): 518–35.

39 Rosa, *Social Acceleration*, 13.

40 Chapter 2 of this book lays out Ricoeur's main arguments about time and then presents an immanent critique of them. Paul Ricoeur, *Time and Narrative*, vol. 1, trans. Kathleen McLaughlin and David Pellauer (Chicago: University of Chicago Press, 1984).

meaningful sequence. The narration of the time of our lives and the time of history must also make use of "reflective instruments" that connect the world of human action to the time of the cosmos. Among them, he lists clocks, calendars, and the concept of generations. The configuration and distribution of time is facilitated by these instruments, or temporal tools, which are conceptual and cultural, as well as tangible. The *poiesis* of time opens the door to a politics of time because temporality is never fixed and is always open to (re)narration. Ricoeur acknowledged the political stakes of temporality at the end of the third volume of *Time and Narrative*, but he touches only on the surface of the issue. This book is an attempt to demonstrate just how deep the politics of time go.

In the following chapters, I propose to organize my exploration of the politics of time around the discussion of a concrete case: the recent debates about reparations for slavery and colonialism. This method of elaboration is, I think, justified because so many of the best-known arguments against reparations proposals make strong claims about temporality. Indeed, it is surprising how often temporal arguments are invoked especially by the opponents of reparations. The chapters all begin by addressing one of the most recurrent criticisms of reparations for slavery and colonialism and then proceed to discussing the politics of time that it entails and upon which it rests.

Perhaps the most common argument against reparations is formulated as an exhortation to focus on the needs of the present instead of dwelling on the past; an obvious point it would seem, at least to those who make such statements. But the idea that we are living in a shared historical epoch, with manifest and indisputable characteristics and needs, is far from self-evident. The second chapter of this book explains that the present is not a *Zeitgeist* that organically unfolds, instead it is better understood as a narrative configuration that is constructed by historical discourse (though not necessarily by professional historians). This claim is based upon a reading of the concept of the historical present laid out by Ricoeur toward the end of *Time and Narrative*. There we find that the present becomes an act of narration that articulates a relationship to a so-called historical community and which involves ethical and political commitments. Although Ricoeur did not dwell on the issue, his analysis leads to the conclusion presented here that the present is not a transparent and neutral firm ground which we can use to circumscribe our practical and political discussions; on the contrary, the construction of narratives of the present must be understood as part of the political contest. After emphasizing the constructivist implications of Ricoeur's argument, the chapter challenges his view by juxtaposing it to the writings of Jacques Rancière. It goes on to suggest that the historical present is often deployed as a mechanism for *interpellating* historical subjects, amenable to the imperatives of the powerful. In other words, the historical present can function as an ideological category. The implications of this theoretical argument are then made clear by showing how different historical presents have been deployed to frame incidents of lethal police violence in the United States.

The third chapter moves on to tackle the standard moral objection to reparations for slavery exemplified so clearly in the words of former French president Nicolas Sarkozy: "No one can ask sons to repent for the mistakes of their fathers." Many would doubtless agree. But the reparations debates have invited a great deal of reflection on the issue of what some philosophers call intergenerational justice. One of the central questions in this discussion has been what—if anything—can we be bound to do because of what previous generations have done? The chapter starts by reviewing some of the influential arguments that have been made about this very question, drawing on the work of Iris Marion Young, Janna Thompson, and others. Yet I do not intend to follow the lead of these philosophers and contribute to the development of a normative theory of intergenerational relations. Principles of intergenerational transmission are indeed important temporal tools—and, in that sense, it is important to get them right. But reparations activists are not at all putting forward proposals for a new morality of intergenerational relations; rather, they are calling upon existing ideas that have been handed down for centuries in the traditions of the West. The third chapter argues that there has long been a conflict between two principles of heredity. The view that Sarkozy espouses, in which it is unjust to burden current generations with the sins of the past, has always existed alongside precisely the opposite view: Not only can responsibility (or indeed punishment) for misdeeds of the past generations be passed down, it is passed down, whether we like it or not. The chapter reviews the history of such ideas from the Greek notion of what classicist Renaud Gagné has called "ancestral fault," and in Biblical discussions of the idea of original sin and the Hamitic curse. I explore the work of intellectual historians who have written about the critique of the doctrine of original sin as being a turning point in Western thought and go on to argue that the idea of inherited responsibility was recast in the language of national belonging and capitalist money with the rise of that new mode of production. This historical analysis sets the stage for a broader discussion of money in chapter 4, where I attempt to illustrate how money functions as a key instrument of temporality today.

Critics of reparations—as well as many who are sympathetic to that cause—admonish proponents for attempting to ascribe monetary value to ineffable suffering, seeing this as both vulgar and impossible. But the proper target of this variety of criticism is not reparations claims per se, but the conception of money and value that such claims would appear to require. That conception is what economic anthropologists call general-purpose money and is, in fact, the dominant understanding of money and value in contemporary capitalist societies.

Under capitalism, most things can be priced. They can thereby be rendered commensurable with all other commodities available on the market. General-purpose money has been used to compare to time itself. In chapter 4, I examine several attempts that have been made to calculate the cost of reparations for slavery and make some critical observations about them: First, the translation of past events into current prices is an anachronistic exercise, one that points to a contradiction between the time of history and the time of economics. While anachronism, in the words of Marc Bloch, constitutes a cardinal "sin" for historians, comparing values across time is virtue itself to the financier. Second, calculating the cost of slavery by applying tools of financial accounting, such as present value calculations, to some wage rate implies the dubious view that a morally acceptable situation would have been one in which the enslaved worked on plantations as low-paid wage laborers. Thirdly, these discussions are rooted in a fetishistic understanding of money and use the language of mainstream economics and finance. This makes pragmatic sense, to be sure, but it still seems odd that attempts to quantify historical exploitation should rely upon the idiom of the exploiter to do so. What would a radical accounting (or audit) of contemporary capitalism look like if it were to start from the point of view of the source of value in labor? For Marx, money was a temporal instrument which rendered the concrete labor of individuals commensurable units of abstract labor, synchronizing and coordinating the activity of people around the world for the production of value. This chapter looks for conceptual tools that could be used to calculate past value in the work of contemporary Marxian, feminist, and environmental thinkers. Of course, I admit from the start that such an accounting could never be carried out in practice, and it would suffer from many of the same moral problems conventional methods face. But considering what a value-based accounting should involve is an important intellectual exercise that can point to new ways to conceptualize the impact of past exploitation on contemporary capitalism. Finally, the exercise is intended to reveal how dominant conceptions of money facilitate fetishistic views of linear historical development. The historically specific form of money and finance that developed with the capitalist mode of production served to homogenize time, by rendering it subject to measurement in money terms, and producing an expectation of "progress" in order to meet the financialized horizon of expectations of the emergent capitalist classes.

The fifth chapter turns to the future, and to the question of how "race" functions as a temporal tool. Here, I begin by discussing John Torpey's famous argument that reparations politics are fundamentally retrospective and arose in order to fill the void left by the decline of emancipatory, utopian political movements. For Torpey, the new politics of the past is indicative of the decline of the future. Arguments of this type have been reiterated in a number of different contexts and have an intuitive appeal. They appear to be in harmony with a broader discourse on postmodernism and presentism. Giving credence to this story, however, would require one to overlook the obvious fact that many proponents of slavery reparations are actually advocating a social-symbolic transformation on a revolutionary scale. Reparations politics, in their most utopian form, asks us to consider the question of the possibility of a solution of the problem of racism: a future without racial oppression.

The feasibility of any such a solution necessarily depends on an accurate understanding of the nature of the problem. On the one hand, the "color-blind" approach focuses on the symbolic dimension of racism and leaves the material underpinnings untouched. On the other hand, purely economic approaches to rectifying racial inequality have been criticized for underestimating the deep penetration of racist conceptions into the symbolic systems of contemporary cultures and psychology of individuals. The term "structural racism" is often used to denote the imbrication of "symbolic" and "material" components of racism today. However, there is no consensus on the precise definition of the term.

Loïc Wacquant, writing in the *New Left Review,* has proposed an alternative sociological framework for understanding the dynamics of "ethnoracial domination" across multiple societies.[41] That model, while useful, can be enriched, I suggest, by adopting the insights of Stuart Hall, in particular his argument about "race" being a floating signifier whose semantic content is shaped by social relations. Adding this perspective is essential because it also underscores the diachronic dimensions of racial oppression and explains how ethnoracial domination reproduces itself across time. Racialization, I argue, has always been a temporal instrument, and this is precisely why it is so persistent.

Both historical and sociological literature have documented how dark skin has been invested with symbolic content by discriminatory practices. What Barbara Fields and Karen Fields call "racecraft" has been centuries in the making.[42] But the call for reparations asks us to consider the opposite process: It asks the question of how a society can deliberately evacuate the semantic content from a sign. In other words, how, in the language of American legal parlance, can we do away with "the badges and incidents of slavery"?

The sixth and concluding chapter argues that this cannot happen within a liberal capitalist framework. I agree that a class-based analysis is essential to any serious attempt to understand the current mode of production and ethnoracial domination. But emancipatory projects wishing to move beyond capitalism must still confront the question that is at the heart of reparations talk: How has this system survived from generation to generation, and how can its vicious cycle be broken? How has what Cedric Robinson names "racial capitalism" persisted for so long? This is the problem once described by Henri Lefebvre as the survival of capitalism. My argument is that reproduction of the relations of production and ethnoracial domination has been achieved, among other ways, by the use of the instruments of temporality that I discuss throughout the book. Many calls for reparations have sought to

41 Loïc Wacquant, "Resolving the Trouble with 'Race,'" *New Left Review* 133 (2022): 67–88.

42 Karen E. Fields and Barbara J. Fields, *Racecraft: The Soul of Inequality in American Life* (London: Verso, 2012).

appropriate those tools of power for different ends. To break this cycle, however, we need new temporalities.

Before I begin these analyses, it is necessary to first say something about the history of the reparations debates. This is no easy task however, because the historiography of the phenomenon forms part of the debates themselves. The investigation into the politics of time I propose must, therefore, begin with an examination of a case of a conflict of historical narration; one in which historians compete to explain reparations claims as either a postmodern form of retrospective politics on the one hand, or as the most recent phase of a long-term struggle for justice on the other.

Reparations talk: A debate across boarders

"[The] history of reparations for slavery would be a history of a nonevent."[43] Robert Westley's description of what slavery reparations litigation had achieved before 2005 remains accurate today in that most concrete proposals have either been ignored or failed to overcome the considerable legal and political obstacles thrown in their way. Indeed, the lack of progress after decades of activism, argument, and legal action is one of the most notable things about the slavery reparations phenomenon. Even so, these obstructed proposals and spurned calls have clearly had a large impact in societies with historical links to slavery by shedding light on, and generating intense public discussion about, the nature and historical origins of contemporary relations of power. In that sense the reparations debates constitute, at the very least—*pace* Westley—a significant discursive event.

Alfred Brophy noted in 2008 already that "reparations talk," by which he meant the proliferation of allusions to the broad theme of addressing the injustices of slavery, had permeated public discourse in the United States and was much more widespread than individual lawsuits or concrete proposals for reparations.[44] This, too, remains an accurate

43 Robert Westley, "The Accursed Share: Genealogy, Temporality, and the Problem of Value in Black Reparations Discourse," *Representations* 92 (2005): 83.

44 Alfred L. Brophy, *Reparations: Pro and Con* (Oxford: Oxford University Press, 2008), xi.

description of the current status of the discussion. In fact, the debate about reparations has only grown in prominence. This book analyzes the politics of time within "reparations talk." Studying a broad debate (instead of a particular proposal or a movement) necessarily involves the hermeneutic exercise of tracing the discursive context in which arguments have been formulated. It requires, therefore, examining different sides of the discussion and analyzing the emergence of anti-reparations talk as an integral part of the same discursive event.

A second consequence of focusing on reparations talk is that it demands that one eschew any normative definition of reparations politics. Instead, it requires being attentive to the wide variety of ways in which reparations have been portrayed. There is no clear and universally embraced definition of them, which, in fact, is one of the main issues of contention in the debates. Critics of reparations usually define them, in the narrowest terms, as a policy of cash payments. In fact, advocates have proposed to use any funds to finance an extremely wide array of policies ranging from scholarships to cultural and educational projects, cooperative enterprises, the protection of Brazilian *quilombos*, the restitution of objects, and more. Some even hold that reparations should be purely symbolic and not involve money at all. Sometimes repair is spoken about in therapeutic or theological terms as a time of healing, a moment of justice, or of "racial reckoning." At other times they are presented as only a means to an end—a source of funds that could be used to pursue other projects such as self-determination and the foundation of new nations, or to foster the economic development of existing ones.

Not only is there no consensus on what precise form reparations should take, there are also different opinions about the injustice they ought to repair. In many countries, it is common to talk of reparations for slavery and colonialism in the same breath. In the US, reparations for slavery are conventionally spoken of together with Jim Crow and contemporary forms of discrimination that have historical roots. Meanwhile, in a Caribbean context, the chair of the CARICOM Reparations Commission, the historian Hilary Beckles, writes of reparations for "slavery and Native Genocide" in combined terms.[45] And there

45 Hilary Beckles, *Britain's Black Debt: Reparations for Caribbean Slavery and Native Genocide* (Kingston: University of the West Indies Press, 2013).

are numerous instances of calls for reparations that make no mention of slavery at all.

This brings me to my third reason for focusing on reparations talk: It has evidently become an increasingly transnational debate. When Brophy coined the phrase, he was speaking of the United States, the country that remains the main reference point in these discussions. But the "talk" is audible within several countries with historical links to slavery and in international venues. France, Spain, Britain, Sweden, Portugal, the Netherlands, Denmark, Romania, and the Vatican have all faced calls for reparations for slavery. There is a lively reparations discussion across several Latin American countries, especially in Brazil and Colombia. Italy, Germany, and Belgium face calls for reparation for their colonial-era atrocities. Turkey and Iran now also face increasing criticism by activists for their historical role in slavery, in addition to other historical misdeeds. Japan has faced compensation demands for sexual slavery and forced labor during World War II. Many more countries have faced claims for other historical crimes.[46] And if reparations advocates have collaborated and conversed across borders, so too have their critics. Anti-reparations talk now appears to have become a transnational repertoire of rebuttals. In this seemingly global Trumpian moment, reparations have become a favorite topic of discussion among right-wing pundits and political groups, who present them as evidence of an anti-Western campaign that has gone too far and must be stopped.

One of the favorite arguments in that discourse goes something like this: "Why don't you ask the Arabs to pay reparations for slavery? They had a larger slave trade than we did." It is a good question, to be sure, and it is one to which there is a simple answer—namely, that they *were* asked. The Arab League faced calls for slavery reparations as early as 2003. At the same time, there have been many calls to discuss racism and the legacies

46 See also Jacqueline Bhabha, Margareta Matache, and Caroline Elkins, *Time for Reparations: A Global Perspective* (Philadelphia: University of Pennsylvania Press, 2021). The First Pan-African Conference on Reparations was held in Abuja, Nigeria, April 27–29, 1993; see inosaar.llc.ed.ac.uk. Reparations were a major issue in the World Conference Against Racism (WCAR) also known as Durban 1 in 2001. In 2022, the Advancing Justice: Reparations and Racial Healing Summit was held in Accra, Ghana, with financing by the MacArthur Foundation; see accrasummit.com. The secretary general of the United Nations, António Guterres, has also recently called for reparations. Catarina Demony, "UN Chief Calls for Slavery Reparations to Overcome 'Generations of Discrimination,'" Reuters, March 25, 2024, reuters.com.

of slavery within the Arabic-speaking world.[47] And in these discussions, a favorite refrain among those who oppose the idea goes something like this: "Slavery under Islam was not as bad as in the Atlantic world, where they had vastly more slaves."[48] Shifting the blame onto others is thus a

47 Daniel Tetteh Osabu-Kle called for reparations in his article "The African Reparation Cry: Rationale, Estimate, Prospects, and Strategies," *Journal of Black Studies* 30, no. 3 (2000). For other examples, see Hisham Aïdi, "Slavery, Genocide and the Politics of Outrage," *MERIP* 234 (Spring 2005): 331–50; or more recently, staff reporter, "Arabs and the West Must Pay for Slavery, Says Pan-African Congress," *Mail and Guardian*, January 23, 2014, mg.co.za. For a recent discussion of the memory of slavery in Tunisia, see, for example, M'hamed Oualdi, "The Politics of Commemorating the Abolition of Slavery in Post-Revolutionary Tunisia," *Middle East Report* 299 (Summer 2021), merip.org. For an interesting study of Morocco, see Chouki El Hamel, *Black Morocco: A History of Slavery, Race, and Islam* (Cambridge: Cambridge University Press, 2013). An important recent lecture discussed a number of countries: Ahmad Sikainga, "Debating Slavery in the Middle East: Perspectives from the Region," lecture, Institute for Comparative Modernities, Cornell University, Ithaca, NY, April 15, 2021, icm.as.cornell.edu. For some examples of media discussions on racism and the legacies of slavery, see: "'Irth al-ʿubūdīyah': Fuṣūl mansīyah min tārīkh al-Maghrib [The legacy of slavery: Forgotten chapters from Moroccan History], al-Araby al-Jadeed, January 4, 2019, alaraby.co.uk; Karfa Sira Diallo, "Le Maghreb: Indifférent à la mémoire de l'esclavage," *Mémoires et partages*, January 23, 2017, memoiresetpartages.com; Sudania 24 TV, "Taʿarraḍt li-mawāqif ʿunṣurīyah min muʿallimatī.. wa-hādhā mā jaʿalat ummī tuʿāniqu-nī wa-tabkī—Sālūn Sūdānīyah—Ḥāl al-balad," YouTube, May 8, 2018, youtube.com; "Webinar Series: Anti-Black Racism in SWANA + Diaspora," *Mizna*, July 24, 2020, mizna.org. Mauritania, infamous for its very belated abolition of slavery, has also proposed to provide reparations. Ibrahim Sylla, "Mauritania's Parliament Passes Law Banning Slavery," Reuters, August 9, 2007, reuters.com. Muammar Gaddafi may have been the second head of state (after President Mathieu Kérékou of Benin in 1999) to ever issue a formal apology—as opposed to an expression of regret, remorse, or sorrow—for slavery when he condemned the role of Arabs in the slave trade in Sirte in 2010.

48 It is not my intention to enter into the very problematic polemic about the extent or severity of slavery in different regions. Those interested in the way scholarship has sought to quantify slavery in the Arabic-speaking world do well to start by reading Gwyn Campbell's review of the literature on this topic: Gwyn Campbell, "Africa and Slavery in the Indian Ocean World," *Africa and the Indian Ocean World from Early Times to Circa 1900*, New Approaches to African History (Cambridge: Cambridge University Press, 2019), 255–80. As he makes clear, these attempts at quantification have been plagued by dubious methods and presuppositions. Also see Mahmood Mamdani, "Introduction: Trans-African Slaveries: Thinking Historically," *Comparative Studies of South Asia, Africa and the Middle East* 38, no. 2 (2018): 185–210. What is beyond dispute, however, is that slavery was significant in its scope and extent across most societies in history. One notable exception to this is the relative absence of slavery from Western Europe in the high Middle Ages. For an interesting explanation of why this came about, see Jeffrey Fynn-Paul, "Empire, Monotheism and Slavery in the Greater Mediterranean Region from Antiquity to the Early Modern Era," *Past and Present* 205, no. 1 (2009): 3–40.

preferred tactic in the East as well as the West, and the right wing in both regions have more in common than they would like to admit.

Providing an adequate historical account of the question of reparations and how it has spread globally as an idea is not a simple task, and I will not attempt it here. But those scholars—other than Westley—who have attempted it, have usually used one of two narrative strategies: In one telling, calls for reparations for slavery are said to be a relatively recent political phenomenon, emerging most forcefully at the end of the twentieth century. In a second, reparations are presented as part of a larger social movement for justice for enslaved people and their descendants, which has waxed and waned but never disappeared from political life. These alternative narratives also tend to frame the stakes and the value of reparations politics in different ways. Histories of reparations, like so much academic writing on the debates about reparations for slavery, form part of the debates themselves. Scholarship has always been at the center of the reparations debates, not on the periphery looking in.

Some have sought to emphasize the recentness of the reparations phenomenon (as per the first narrative) in order to make the claim that it is a postmodern form of politics characterized by a peculiar relationship to time. What is notable about this type of activism—so these scholars say—is that the past, not the future, is the focus of political energies. Reparations claims are to be explained by viewing them within the context of a "memory wave" that has been sweeping through the world. Memory has become an urgent political issue in a new way as movements for the commemoration apology, redress, and reparation for historical misdeeds (not only slavery) have sprung up all over the globe in recent years.

These developments have been welcomed by some, such as Elazar Barkan, who has suggested that the proliferation of such movements marks the emergence of what he dubs a "Neo-Enlightenment morality" accompanying a more general growth in commitment to human rights.[49] But others are more critical of the turn to the past, which they see as connected to an abandonment of the future-oriented political ideas that characterized the twentieth century. Among the most prominent voices on the American left to articulate similar views have been Adolph Reed

49 Elazar Barkan, *The Guilt of Nations: Restitution and Negotiating Historical Injustices* (Baltimore: Johns Hopkins University Press, 2001).

Jr., Touré Reed, and Walter Benn Michaels. Their stance is that reparations politics are pernicious, and instead, they advocate for a return to a more broad-based, class-focused political action. Wendy Brown, like John Torpey, has also argued that this rise of the politics of the past is the result of a decline of the future and the emergence of identity politics or the politics of recognition. What these authors mean is that the abandonment of progressive narratives of emancipation—particularly those offered by socialism, the Civil Rights Movement, and, for Brown, the meta-narrative of liberalism—has led to a search for new political goals.[50] As a consequence, people have turned inward toward their own groups and to the past. "When the future collapses the past rushes in."[51]

Scholars like Pierre Nora, and others have—as we saw earlier—presented reparations as a symptom of a broader societal pathology. The malaise caused by the acceleration of events in the presentist regime of historicity has resulted in people turning to memory and toward the past. In French discussions, memory has been firmly linked to the threat of *communautarisme*, in a manner that resembles the debates about identity politics in the anglophone world. The rise of couple memory / *communautarisme* (characterized as divisive, identity-obsessed, and irrational) is said to come at the cost of a diminution of history / the French Republic (which are presented as universal, inclusive, and rational). Here, too, the postmodern abandonment of the grand narratives and the concomitant loss of hope in the future are to blame.[52]

Similar ideas are put in even more provocative terms by the writer Pascal Bruckner, who claims that the focus on the past has become a source of resentment. He decries what he calls the tyranny of repentance across the West.[53] His critique of the penchant for "auto-flagellation" has been taken up by a number of prominent French public intellectuals as well as politicians.[54] Nicolas Sarkozy expressed his condemnation of this

50 I discuss this in detail in the fifth chapter of this book.

51 John Torpey, *Making Whole What Has Been Smashed: On Reparations Politics* (New Brunswick, NJ: Rutgers University Press, 2017).

52 This argument is elaborated in more detail in Van de Mieroop, "The 'Age of Commemoration' as a Narrative Construct."

53 Pascal Bruckner, *La Tyrannie de la pénitence: Essai sur le masochisme occidental* (Paris: Grasset, 2006), 19. His book was translated into English under the title *The Tyranny of Guilt: An Essay on Western Masochism*, trans. Steven Rendall (Princeton, NJ: Princeton University Press, 2010).

54 Louis-Georges Tin lists some of the most important names: "In the political

trend in no uncertain terms: "I hate this repentance which is a falsification of the history of France. Because France should not be ashamed of its history."[55] Across Europe and North America politicians, commentators and academics have insisted that reparations are part of a general culture of "wokeness" that poses a grave threat to the West by dictating that there is nothing to be proud of in the region's history and the only acceptable position on the past is one of repentance.[56]

A longer view of the history of reparations

But "who said anything about repentance?" Rosa Amelia Plumelle-Uribe points out that

> what African patriots want and what they seek—until now by peaceful means—is not the repentance of Europeans but the end of their interventionist policy in Africa. And also the restitution of at least a small part of the incalculable wealth looted from this continent.[57]

---

sphere, Nicolas Sarkozy, Christian Vanneste, or Jean-Marie Le Pen; in the media sphere, Alain Finkelkraut, Éric Zemmour, or Ivan Rioufol." *Esclavage et Réparations* (Paris: Stock, 2013), 50 (my translation).

55 "Tel quel: Sarkozy: 'Je déteste la repentance,'" *L'Humanité*, May 10, 2007, humanite.fr (my translation).

56 See, for example, Gwythian Prins, "The Historical Roots of 'Wokery': Of What Is This an Instance?," History Reclaimed, February 14, 2022, historyreclaimed.co.uk. Douglas Murray has been very influential and his book, *The Strange Death of Europe: Immigration, Identity, Islam* (London: Bloomsbury Publishing, 2017), was translated into German, French, Italian, and Japanese.

57 She continues: "As for the descendants of Africans deported to the Americas, whether they are South American, North American, or from Central America and the Caribbean, the activists advocating for reparations whom I have met have never spoken about repentance and we have not addressed the subject. That is because they have other priorities, like finding effective mechanisms to correct the negative effects of anti-Black racism, which is itself a consequence of the slave trade and the enslavement of Black people. They do not speak of repentance, only of implementing a policy of reparation. In reality, the controversy for or against repentance is a false debate invented to sidestep the real issue that some find troubling, namely, a discussion about the forms a policy of reparation could take and how to implement it." Rosa Amelia Plumelle-Uribe, *Traite des blancs, traites des noirs: Aspects méconnus et conséquences actuelles* (Paris: L'Harmattan, 2010), 198 (my translation). In fact, as I will go on to argue later in this book, the language of "repentance" for the "original sin" of slavery is mostly typical of liberal advocates of reparations for slavery in the United States and is usually absent from the discourse of radical and nationalist groups.

Plumelle-Uribe, who is also an activist, is one of the many scholars who present a sympathetic view of the reparations phenomenon that is also grounded in a more intimate knowledge of the content of reparations claims. Such accounts tend to use the second narrative strategy, placing reparations movements at the center of the discussion. These scholars usually also widen the chronological context to show that slavery reparations are best understood as one instance of a larger and ongoing struggle for justice in a world system marked by clear inequalities of power and wealth. Ana Lucia Araujo's history of the reparations movements illustrates that the calls for redress and compensation can already be found in the eighteenth century in the United States.[58] The prominence of the American case in reparations talk today is due, in the first place, to the pole position of American media in the production and distribution of cultural products in the global economy. But it also the result of the long history of movements for redress in that country. Many say that the first reparations lawsuit, *Johnson v. McAdoo*, dates to 1915.[59] Araujo shows, however, that already in 1778, Pompey Brakkee sued his former owner and won £400 compensation.[60]

Recent demands for reparations are a new iteration of an old idea. Dashed promises of "forty acres and a mule" made to the Freedmen were never forgotten.[61] Robin D. G. Kelley explains that each generation since the end of the Civil War has requested some sort of material

58 Ana Lucia Araujo, *Reparations for Slavery and the Slave Trade: A Transnational and Comparative History* (London: Bloomsbury, 2017), 7. Her transnational approach to the study of the issue is so valuable because the majority of scholarship on reparations focuses on one specific country, and, as I have said, the United States remains at the center of most discussions.

59 John G. Browning, "Seeking the Fruits of Their Labors: The Story of *Johnson v. McAdoo*, the First Major Reparations Case," *Journal of Race, Gender, and Ethnicity* 11, no. 1 (2022).

60 Araujo, *Reparations for Slavery and the Slave Trade*, 48.

61 The phrase "forty acres and a mule" refers to General Sherman's Special Field Order Number 15 of January 1865 issued at the end of the Civil War, which reserved land in the Confederate South for freed slaves. The land was to be divided into parcels of forty acres. Eventually, however, the land was returned to its former white owners and the plans for redistribution were abandoned. Henceforth, "forty acres and a mule" has been a recurring trope in American political discourse over generations and refers to unkept promises and the idea that a debt has been owed to the formerly enslaved and their descendants but has never been paid.

compensation for slavery but has seen its calls rebuffed.[62] Sometimes, this idea took the form of concrete policies such as slave pensions.[63] At other times, the language of unpaid debts was used to support other polices—as when Martin Luther King Jr. referred to America's promissory note in his iconic speech during the March on Washington in 1963. But calls for reparation proper predate that: In 1957 Audley Moore presented a petition to the United Nations for reparations. And in 1969, after King's speech, James Forman, former member of the SNCC, wrote the Black Manifesto, also calling for financial compensation. In the 1970s and '80s, groups like the Republic of New Africa and the African People's Socialist Party demanded reparations as a way of financing anti-capitalist projects.[64]

Many scholars agree that, after a high point in the 1990s, media interest in reparations began to die down in the aftermath of September 11, 2001. But Ta-Nehisi Coates is credited with reigniting it in the pages of the *Atlantic* in 2014. His disquisition also took a longer view of the issue, drawing a connection from slavery to Jim Crow, down through to housing discrimination in the present.[65] Coates's article was widely discussed in countries around the world, not just in the US. By the time of the run-up to the 2020 presidential election in the United States, the main Democratic candidates were asked about their position on the issue of reparations. One year earlier, the *New York Times* launched its 1619 Project with the professed goal of placing slavery at the heart of the mainstream narrative of American history and illustrating the continuity

62 Robin D. G. Kelley, "'A Day of Reckoning': Dreams of Reparations," in Michael T. Martin and Marilyn Yaquinto, eds., *Redress for Historical Injustices in the United States: On Reparations for Slavery, Jim Crow, and Their Legacies* (Durham, NC: Duke University Press, 2007).

63 Mary Frances Berry, "Reparations for Freedmen, 1890–1916: Fraudulent Practices or Justice Deferred?," *Journal of Negro History* 57, no. 3 (1972).

64 In 1972 the RNA presented their "Anti-Depression Program of the Republic of New Africa" to Congress. The plan called for the establishment of a new African nation that would reject "laissez-faire capitalism" and instead embrace the cooperative principles of *Ujamma*, based on the Tanzanian model under Julius Nyerere. See "The Anti-Depression Program of the Republic of New Africa," reprinted in William L. Van Deburg, *Modern Black Nationalism: from Garvey to Louis Farrakhan* (New York: NYU Press, 1997), 197. See also Omali Yeshitela, *Stolen Black Labor: The Political Economy of Domestic Colonialism* (Oakland, CA.: Burning Spear, 1983).

65 Ta-Nehisi Coates, "The Case for Reparations," *Atlantic*, May 21, 2014, theatlantic .com.

of racist oppression in the country up until the present day. The leading journalist involved in the project, Nikole Hannah-Jones, also called for reparations.

Demonstrating that demands for reparations have not come out of the blue, but actually go back a long way, has another advantage: It helps to counter one of the main legal barriers to reparations lawsuits, the statute of limitations or the time bar. The legal arguments about whether to toll the time bar are perhaps the most obvious example of the politics of time at the heart of the reparations debates. This temporal tool limits the amount of time during which legal action can be taken. Plaintiffs in reparations cases have had to argue that the statute of limitations should be equitably tolled. This is to say, the court has discretion to "stop the clock" on the time bar if it is clear that the plaintiffs were unable to bring suit in the time of limitation. Reparations advocates have thus commonly argued that potential plaintiffs were unable to seek justice in American courts during the period after slavery and during Jim Crow when racial oppression was still firmly in place.[66] But this argument has not been successful in court.

Even though calls for compensation go far back, most observers agree that the success of Japanese Americans in obtaining reparations for incarceration in the Civil Liberties Act of 1988, and the strong push by the American government to pursue further Holocaust reparations, inspired many activists to bring up the question of reparations for slavery in the American Congress and in the courts during the 1990s. Yet all those reparations lawsuits for slavery failed, and Representative John Conyers's bill HR 40, which proposed to establish a commission to study the issue, only made it out of committee for the first time in 2021, even though it had been introduced every year since 1989.

In a 1995 legal case, *Cato v. the United States*, the plaintiff sought to circumvent the problem of statute of limitations by referring to the principal of "continuing violations." In other words, Cato contended that African Americans continue to face discrimination, police brutality, and

66 This point has been argued by a number of legal scholars, including Robert Westley. See also Eric J. Miller, "Representing the Race: Standing to Sue in Reparations Lawsuits," *Harvard Blackletter Law Journal* 91 (2004); Kaimipono David Wenger, "Causation and Attenuation in the Slavery Reparations Debate," *University of San Francisco Law Review* 40 (2005–6); Suzette M. Malveaux, "Statutes of Limitations: A Policy Analysis in the Context of Reparations Litigation," *George Washington Law Review* 68 (2005–6).

lack of democratic representation in government, and that they are still "subjected to the badges and indicia of slavery." But the court was not convinced. It ruled that "without a concrete, personal injury that is not abstract and that is fairly traceable to the government conduct that she challenges as unconstitutional, Cato lacks standing."[67] The logic of the ruling puts the onus on those demanding reparations to illustrate the continuation of harms over generations and appears to imply that the passage of time erodes or attenuates injustice.

A French court in Fort-de-France presented similar reasoning when deciding against the case brought by the Mouvement International pour les Réparations (MIR) against the French state; the court found it *irrecevable*, inadmissible. The MIR attempted to argue that slavery had been deemed a crime against humanity by the Taubira law of 2001, and because crimes against humanity are imprescriptible, no time limit should apply. In support of the initial decision, the *court de cassation* later noted that the Taubira law did not, in fact, mean that the crime was imprescriptible—a highly significant interpretation that went against what many would see as the whole point of the law.[68] It also cast doubt on the question of intergenerational transmission:

67 On Cato's lack of standing, see also the following statement: "No plaintiff has standing 'to complain simply that their Government is violating the law.' Id. at 755. Neither does Cato have standing to litigate claims based on the stigmatizing injury to all African Americans caused by racial discrimination. Id. In any case, she does not trace the presence of discrimination and its harm to the United States rather than to other persons or institutions. Accordingly, Cato lacks standing to bring a suit setting forth the claims she suggests." *Cato v. United States*, nos. 94-17102, 94-17104, United States Court of Appeals, Ninth Circuit, December 4, 1995, caselaw.findlaw.com.

68 "Articles 211-1 and 212-1 of the Penal Code, which punish crimes against humanity, entered into force on March 1, 1994, and cannot apply to acts committed prior to that date due to the principles of legality of offenses and penalties and of non-retroactivity of stricter penal laws; that the law of May 21, 2001 [the Taubira law], did not attenuate these principles; that the civil action brought against the State, independently of any criminal classification, was subject both to the statute of limitations under former Article 2262 of the same code and to the forfeiture of claims against the State provided for in Article 9 of the law of January 29, 1831, now Article 1 of the law of December 31, 1968; that the court of appeal had therefore correctly held that this action, insofar as it concerned acts that ended in 1848, and despite the suspension of the statute of limitations until the day the victims or their beneficiaries were able to act, was time-barred in the absence of demonstration of an impediment which would have lasted for more than 100 years." *Communique de presse mir et autres contre Etat français*, Cour d'appel de Fort-de-France, January 18, 2022, la1ere.francetvinfo.fr (my translation).

> The only references to transgenerational damage linked to the influence of the human environment on genetics and the existence of phenomena of transmission of historic collective traumas of a dehumanizing nature, and also to material damage and morals experienced by all the descendants of slaves did not make it possible to establish for each of the natural persons the existence of a certain, direct, and personal prejudice in connection with the transatlantic slave trade and slavery.[69]

Both findings describe the connection between litigants in the present day and the historical crimes of slavery as abstract, precisely the view that many historians have tried to counter by illustrating the continuities of different forms of exploitation, violence, and discrimination.

For a long time, legal scholars have suggested that reparations cases would meet with more success if they sought compensation for more recent crimes. In the so-called Mau Mau case, victims of torture at the hands of the British during the uprisings in Kenya during the 1950s did succeed in winning compensation. In 2024, a court in Brussels found the Belgian government guilty of crimes against humanity in a case brought by five women who were forcibly abducted from Congo in their childhood.[70] The Dutch government had to offer compensation to the children of Indonesians executed in the war of independence. In France, the Conseil représentatif des associations noires (CRAN) has called for reparations for the Thiaroye massacre and the construction of the Congo-Ocean train line with forced labor. Countless other colonial-era demands remain to be addressed.

But proximity in time is no guarantee of success. In the United States, the Reparations Coordination Commission (RCC) carefully designed a legal strategy to obtain reparations for the Tulsa massacre of 1921. RCC sued the State of Oklahoma, the City of Tulsa, the Tulsa Police Department, and the chief of police on behalf of 100 surviving victims. According to Alfred Brophy, the Tulsa case seemed to offer a clear example of when the statute of limitation should be tolled. Because the government was complicit in the crime, victims could not seek justice

69 Ibid. (my translation).

70 "Belgian Ruling a Landmark Win for Reparations Movement," Human Rights Watch, December 3, 2024, hrw.org.

when it occurred.[71] The RCC argued that the statute of limitations should be extended until the time of the publication of the report of the Oklahoma Commission to Study the Race Riot, since before that time a "conspiracy of silence" had made it impossible to bring the case, and the extent of the complicity of the government was not fully known. But the courts denied that the statute of limitations could be tolled this far. In this case, too, the court's reasoning relied on a rather vague historical claim that suggested that the civil rights legislation of the 1960s constituted a turning point:

> While exceptional circumstances may have prevented victims from seeking timely legal redress . . . the emergence of civil rights legislation in the 1960s gave them the ability to do so. In fact, Plaintiffs neither allege nor even imply that they were prohibited from accessing the courts in the 1970s, 1980s, or 1990s.[72]

A temporal argument was thus once again a stumbling block.

Lawsuits by citizens of one country against their own government face all sorts of legal barriers and political obstacles beyond the statute of limitations. But interstate claims face different concerns. This is partly because relations between states are conventionally governed by a different temporality from that governing relations between individuals, a topic I explore in chapter 3. Interstate claims are considered a serious threat by those countries from whom they are being demanded. This was clear to see in the late summer of 2001 in the run-up to the World Conference Against Racism in Durban, South Africa.[73] During numerous preparatory meetings, African countries raised the issue of reparations for slavery and colonialism on several occasions.[74] The NGO Human Rights Watch also made a powerful case for reparations at that

71 Brophy, *Reparations: Pro and Con*, 131.

72 *Alexander v. State of Oklahoma*, no. 04-5042, US District Court for the Northern District of Oklahoma, September 8, 2004, washburnlaw.edu.

73 Charles P. Henry, *Long Overdue: The Politics of Racial Reparations* (New York: NYU Press, 2007); Martha Biondi, "The Rise of the Reparations Movement," *Radical History Review* 87 (2003): 5–18.

74 The Durban declaration also called for debt relief. *World Conference Against Racism, Racial Discrimination, Xenophobia and Related Intolerance: Declaration and Programme of Action* (New York: United Nations Human Rights, 2002), un.org.

time.[75] The United States walked out of the conference, ostensibly because of the proposed association of Zionism with racism, but many believed that it also had to do with a desire to avoid dealing with the question of reparations. In any case, the American government's decision to send low-level representatives to the conference instead of the secretary of state, Colin Powell, was taken to be a sign of the lack of interest in the issues raised there. The French government also expressed concern about reparations, explaining that instead of dwelling on the past it was best to look to the "future."[76]

A few years later, Jean-Bertrand Aristide, the president of Haiti who had called for France to give back the money that his country had been forced to pay as reparations to slave owners since 1825, was deposed in a coup. In 2022 the *New York Times* reported what many had already suspected: The ouster was organized by France, together with the United States.[77]

75 Human Rights Watch, *An Approach to Reparations* (New York: Human Rights Watch, 2001), hrw.org.

76 Christophe Ayad, "Une patate chaude pour la diplomatie française," *Libération*, August 12, 2001, liberation.fr.

77 Constant Méheut, Catherine Porter, Selam Gebrekidan, and Matt Apuzzo, "The Ransom: Demanding Reparations and Ending Up in Exile," *New York Times*, May 20, 2022, nytimes.com.

2

The Historical Present as an Ideological Category

Nothing says that the present reduces to presence.
—Paul Ricoeur, *Time and Narrative*

The contemporary division between whites and blacks in America arises out of the white conviction that the civil rights movement achieved its antiracist objective and recognized the basic rights of blacks, and the black conviction that despite changes in the law, racism remains the central problem. Many whites do not deny the existence of racism, but view it as greatly abated, more a case of "the way we were" rather than "the way we are now." Blacks, by contrast, tend to see racism as different in appearance today but not in reality; for them, racism may have burrowed underground but it remains deeply embedded in the national psyche and in American institutions.
—Dinesh D'Souza, *The End of Racism*

Critics of reparations sometimes attempt to make the point that historical slavery has minimal relevance to the world today by emphatically stating the number of years that have passed since abolition. Nick Hækkerup, the former Danish minister for trade and Europe, expressed this sentiment when asked to comment about his government's position on the issue: "Slavery is a black and dark chapter in world history," he said, but it is now in the past: "We cannot undo the past . . . What we can, must and will do is to focus on the present and the future."[1] To this relegation of the problem to the past, reparations advocates have responded that they *are* focusing on the present. The legacies of slavery, colonialism, and racism in fact shape the present and will continue to do so into the future if they are not adequately addressed or acknowledged.

At the heart of the reparations debates, then, is a disagreement about the nature of the present. Indeed, all political debates involve statements, whether implicit or explicit, about the state of the present and current affairs. Any assessment of the pressing concerns of our time involves appraising what legacies and unresolved questions from the past must be dealt with and envisioning what challenges are likely to arise in the future. Articulating an account of the present historical moment is, therefore, a crucial part of political discourse and the politics of time. The present is not a firm ground to which we can anchor our discussions; the definition of the present is itself part of the political contest.

Initially, it appears as though different groups and individuals—parties, politicians, pundits, and so on—offer competing descriptions of the current situation and that matters might be settled, at least in part, by deciding which description is more accurate. Yet what is at issue is not so much the description of the present, but rather its narration. That is because, as I will argue in this chapter, the historical present is a narrative category. In other words, when speaking of the historical moment in which we live, we are not simply describing the *Zeitgeist* or the surroundings in which we find ourselves. Rather, we are in the process of constructing a narrative of a particular kind: one that articulates a relationship to a so-called historical community and involves ethical and political commitments. That is, at least, how the philosopher Paul Ricoeur puts it in his expansive philosophical investigation into the topic of temporality *Time and Narrative.*

Ricoeur's reflections on the nature of historicity are necessarily abstract, and his account requires some modification. Upon reflection, it becomes clear that the implicit subject of his hermeneutics of historical consciousness is a citizen of a modern Western nation-state. He does not seriously consider the political consequences of multiple or

1 "Denmark Nixes Slavery Apology, Reparations," *Saint Thomas Source*, December 11, 2013, stthomassource.com; Vinette K. Pryce, "Virgin Islanders Seek Reparations from Denmark," *Caribbean Life*, October 11, 2015, caribbeanlife.com.

subaltern historicities. The argument that follows in this chapter aims to make the issue more concrete, while also demonstrating that it is an even more complex matter than Ricoeur's analysis admits. I attempt to do so by showing that the slavery reparations debates involve a competition between different viable—but by no means equal—narratives of the present historical moment. In this chapter, I analyze three of them. There are, of course, many more, but I have chosen these three because they are among the most recognizable in the United States. I label these the post-racial, the liberal, and the nationalist. I argue that they demonstrate something about historical presents that Ricoeur did not address: They can function as ideological categories.

The historical present

In historiography—professional historical writing—the past is the enigma in need of clarification; the "foreign country" that the historian must seek to explain or understand.[2] The present, on the other hand, is very often treated as if it were a self-evident firm ground upon which observers of the past stand. Alternatively, it is viewed as a problem that requires bracketing: Historians must remain wary of how their situation in time and space might prejudice their reading of the past. Yet the assumption that the present is more transparent and knowable to us than the past is a problematic one. Throughout centuries of philosophical discourse and reflection on time, it is the category of the present that has been the source of great puzzlement and confusion. It is precisely for this reason that Paul Ricoeur begins and concludes his magnum opus with a consideration of the present. And yet, even though *Time and Narrative* has become, by now, a classic text, the category of what Ricoeur calls the "historical present" has received scant attention in the scholarly literature on his oeuvre.[3] This oversight is surprising, since the

2 David Lowenthal, *The Past Is a Foreign Country* (Cambridge: Cambridge University Press, 1985); and *The Past Is a Foreign Country—Revisited* (Cambridge: Cambridge University Press, 2015).

3 There is a vast philosophical literature on Ricoeur's works and an entire journal devoted to the study of this great philosopher. Although the historical present is mentioned in several studies, I was unable to identify any article or book chapter that treats Ricoeur's category as its central topic. Also, in the field of memory studies, the

explication of the historical present in the third volume of *Time and Narrative* can be understood as a resolution of the problems set out in volume 1. As he puts it, the "consideration of the historical present brings to its ultimate stage the reply of thought about history to the aporias of speculation about time, nourished by phenomenology."[4] The question of time begins and ends with the present.

The first aporia Ricoeur refers to—one of the oldest in philosophy—is about the nature of the present.[5] Volume 1 begins by reviewing Aristotle's disquisition in *Physics IV* on the being and nonbeing of time. The "now" is generally considered as the temporal moment that is immediate to us. The future is yet to come, and the past is what has been. The ancient philosopher famously explains that time appears, therefore, to belong to the order of things that do not exist, because the future *is* not yet and the past *is* no longer. To the objection that the now-moment is the part of time that exists, Aristotle responds that when something we can divide is said to exist, a part of it must exist after its division. But this is not the case with the now-moment, which seems to disappear into past and future with every division.

Put another way, when we start to contemplate the instant, we find that it is difficult, if not impossible, to grasp it, because instants flow ceaselessly into the past as fast as we can register them as present. This puzzle has been discussed by philosophers over many generations. Ricoeur shows that previous attempts to resolve it have produced two broad strands of thinking about time in philosophy: One, which we might call the external or cosmological view, presents time as the "number of movement in respect of the before and after"—as Aristotle put it (*Physics* IV 14). Time, in this first view, is linked to movement and to the cosmos. Or, later, it is perceived as a parameter of sorts—as in Newtonian ideas of absolute space and time—that is something independent from the observer. On the other hand, there is a second view,

---

category has been almost completely disregarded. Scholars writing in that field have for the most part preferred to refer to his book *Memory, History, Forgetting* (Chicago: University of Chicago Press, 2004), even though Ricoeur intended that volume as a means of building upon the arguments he had set out in his earlier *Time and Narrative*.

4 Paul Ricoeur, *Time and Narrative*, vol. 3, trans. Kathleen Blamey and David Pellauer (Chicago: University of Chicago Press, 1988), 233.

5 Aristotle raises three "aporias" in his account of time. Here I explain Ricoeur's reconstruction of Aristotle's arguments.

what we could call the internal or phenomenological view, which presents time as an element of human existence or perception; from the idea of the distention of the soul in Augustine, Kant's forms of intuition, through to within-time-ness (*Innerzeitigkeit*) of Heidegger.

The external and internal views each elucidate important aspects of the phenomenon of time, but can we develop a philosophical account that incorporates the important elements of both? The question of how to connect these perspectives presents a second aporia according to Ricoeur. He remains unconvinced by previous philosophical attempts to resolve the problem and devotes particular attention to showing how Martin Heidegger struggled with it. Heidegger, notably, sought to ground what he called the "vulgar" and "flattened" concepts of linear time—which he associated with Aristotle—in something more fundamental, something he called "originary temporality." But this project was unsuccessful, and Heidegger is shown to be "a philosopher with his back to the wall," having written himself into a corner and being unable to find a way out.[6]

Time and Narrative presents an innovative solution to both philosophical problems. It is a poetic rather than logical solution, since it depends on the human capacity to narrate. Time becomes human time to the extent that it is organized after the manner of a narrative; narrative, in turn, is meaningful to the extent that portrays the features of temporal experience.[7]

Narration, a form of *poiesis*, gives the present its "thickness" and significance. Plot structures unite the heterogeneous into a meaningful homogeneity—a "discordant-concordant structure"—and allow us to "grasp . . . together" a diversity of things scattered in time and space.[8] Plots mediate "between the individual events or incidents and a story taken as a whole" and "bring . . . together factors as heterogeneous as agents, goals, means, interactions, circumstances, unexpected results."[9]

6 Ricoeur, *Time and Narrative*, vol. 3, 80.

7 Paul Ricoeur, *Time and Narrative*, vol. 1, trans. Kathleen McLaughlin and David Pellauer (Chicago: University of Chicago Press, 1984), 3.

8 Ricoeur, *Time and Narrative*, vol. 3, 11; Ricoeur, *Time and Narrative*, vol. 1, 65.

9 "A narrative makes appear within a syntagmatic order all the components capable of figuring in the paradigmatic tableau established by the semantics of action. This passage from the paradigmatic to the syntagmatic constitutes the transition from $mimesis_1$ to $mimesis_2$." Ibid., 66. Ricoeur outlines his idea of the threefold mimesis in chapter 3 of *Time and Narrative*, vol. 1. He argues that a hermeneutical approach must

Submitted to emplotment, moments of time may be read forward and backward.[10] And narration bestows a "'sense of an ending' . . . to the indefinite succession of incidents."[11] Endpoints are not simply marks on a calendar or schedule; through narration they become moments of recognition or *anagnorisis*. Ricoeur incorporates humanity's poetic ability into the Heideggerian discourse by raising the capacity to narrate to the level of an "*existentiale*," saying that narrative recounts "care" (*Sorge*). The present then becomes an act of narration, a narrative "making-present" (*Gegenwärtigung*).

Narrative also provides the key to overcoming the impasse that Heidegger wrote himself into when trying to "ground" the external view of time.[12] Ricoeur insists that cosmological time must be given its due as an independent pole of temporality. Instead of trying to derive one from the other, Ricoeur proposes to bridge the two views of time by introducing a third level of temporality, what he calls *historical time*. Historical time is, therefore, a crucial existential category. History holds a central place in his account.[13] It is through historical narration that human lives are imbued with historical significance.

Historical narratives coordinate the lives of individuals with those of others in a "we" relation by referring to what Ricoeur terms "reflective instruments"—what I have also been calling temporal tools or instruments of temporality—such as clocks, calendars, the notion of an axial

---

take account of "the entire arc of operations" whereby a textual configuration (mimesis$_2$) mediates between "the prefiguration of the practical field" (mimesis$_1$) and a moment of "refriguration through the reception of the work" (mimesis$_3$); ibid., 53.

10 "To follow a story is to move forward in the midst of contingencies and peripeteia under the guidance of an expectation that finds its fulfillment in the 'conclusion' of the story. This conclusion is not logically implied by some previous premises. It gives the story an 'end point', which in turn, furnishes the point of view from which the story can be perceived as forming a whole. To understand the story is to understand how and why the successive episodes led to the conclusion, which, far from being foreseeable, must finally be acceptable, as congruent with the episodes brought together by the story." Ibid., 66–7.

11 Ibid., 67.

12 Ricoeur does not think that phenomenological time, the time of human concern, could produce its "polar opposite"; Ricoeur, *Time and Narrative*, vol. 3, 89. For a detailed discussion of the essence of Ricoeur's critique of Heidegger's view on time, see also Françoise Dastur, "La critique ricœurienne de la conception de la temporalité dans Être et temps de Heidegger," *Archives de Philosophie* 74, no. 4 (October 1, 2011): 565–80.

13 This is one of the reasons that Ricoeur is so popular among historians (in France at least), something few philosophers of history have managed to achieve.

moment, documents and traces, and the idea of the succession of generations.[14] To view ourselves in historical time is thus to emplot our lives into a story of a historical community. Following Koselleck, historical time is here understood a "collective singular," or an "eclectic unity" of disparate stories. The configuration of historical narratives in *mimesis*$_2$ leads to a "refiguration" (*mimesis*$_3$) of our lived experiences. We see our lives in a different way when we view them in a historical context because to do so is to submit them to an emplotment that refers to reflective instruments and situates the individual between a "space of experience" (*Erfahrungsraum*) "and the horizon of expectation" (*Erwartungshorizont*) that is shared with a historical community. Koselleck's two categories are transcendental for properly *historical* experience.

The historical present, then, can first of all be understood as a moment of auto-periodization into historical time. It is analogous to the lived present on the level of phenomenological time in that it is not a moment that simply overcomes us but one that requires active configuration, a "making present." Phenomenological time and historical time thus share a narrative quality, but the latter has an essentially public character. Both categories are also moments in which action is initiated, and the historical present is bound up with the concept of "initiative":

> To tie the fate of the present to that of initiative is to subtract the present from the prestige of presence in the quasi-optical sense of the term . . . To restore to making-present an authenticity equal to that of anticipatory resoluteness, I propose to connect the two ideas of making-present and initiative. The present is then, no longer a category of seeing, but one of acting and suffering.[15]

This initiative is directed toward others in the community; it consists in a public declaration:

14 "History initially reveals its creative capacity as regards the refiguration of time through its invention and use of certain reflective instruments such as the calendar; the idea of the succession of generations—and, connected to this, the idea of the threefold realm of contemporaries, predecessors and successors; finally, and above all, in its recourse to the archives, documents and traces. These reflective instruments are noteworthy in that they play the role of connectors between lived time and universal time. In this respect, they bear witness to the poetic function of history insofar as it contributes to solving the aporias of time." Ricoeur, *Time and Narrative*, vol. 3, 104.

15 Ibid., 230.

> Through the "I can," initiative indicates power; through the "I do," it becomes my act; through interference or intervention, it inscribes my act in the course of things, thereby making the lived present coincide with the particular instant, through the kept promise, it gives the present the force of persevering, in short, of enduring. By this last trait, initiative is clothed with an ethical signification that announces the more specifically *political* and cosmopolitan characterization of the historical present.[16]

Statements about the historical present are "commissives" which assign individuals a place in the syntagmatic order of the story of a given historical community. They are assertions of "contemporaneity" that "immediately confers on the historical present the dimension of a we-relation, in virtue of which several flows of consciousness are coordinated in terms of 'growing old together.'"[17] To speak about the historical present always involves making an ethical-political commitment to that community. This commitment is directed to the past and to the future: It consists in taking a stance on the space of experience through the evaluation of what Ricoeur calls "tradition" and making a "promise" to historical community about the horizon of expectation.

Taking a stance on "tradition" thus means reckoning with the complex question of transmission. Ricoeur introduces a tripartite notion of tradition—*traditionality*, *traditions*, and *tradition*—by which he means, respectively, the ongoing dynamic whereby humans are affected by the past but also evaluate the past and effect themselves in history, the "transmission," through "interpretation" and "reinterpretation" of meaning as actions from the past in a language-like manner (*langagière*), and the "legitimation of the claim to truth raised by every heritage that bears meaning."[18] Ricoeur's discussion of the "promise" to the historical community in the horizon of expectation marks the point at which his analysis of the historical present moves, most explicitly, from "the ethical plane to the political one."[19] This is because promises "commit the monadic subject only on the condition of a reciprocity

16 Ibid., 233 (my emphasis).

17 Ibid., 234.

18 Ibid., 221, 228.

19 Ibid., 234.

governing mutual expectations and, in the end, a social pact dependent upon the idea of justice."[20]

If Ricoeur is correct, humans are always reckoning with the question of how to deal with the legacies of the past and making public promises for the future that, in the end, depend upon an idea of justice. In this sense we might say that the question of what to do about the legacies of slavery and colonialism, now and in the future, is simply one case of a more general, and indeed essentially human, matter. It is of central existential significance for humans to orient themselves in a broader historical story. But this still leaves open the question of the right way to do so.

An ideological category

Ricoeur's turn to narrative and his celebration of the poetic resources of the capable human being allowed him to resolve aporias that have frustrated other philosophers for centuries. He reveals that, through narration, the present is transformed from a fleeting instant into an activity full of significance. The historical present is transformed from a temporal background or context in which activities take place into a political category: an activity of self-emplotment into a collective singular story; a moment of evaluation of "tradition" and of promises for the future.

But the invocation of the narrative capacity also brings with it a new set of concerns. Key among these is how to contend with the idea of the unity or oneness of historical time. Ricoeur himself acknowledges that there is a tension between the universal pretension of claims about historical time, and the local and specific character of narratives. He appears to be caught between his insistence that the subject of historical time, the historical community, must be humanity in general, and his recognition that the turn to narrative requires him to renounce any Hegelian attempt to conceive of a "plot behind every plot."[21] *Time and Narrative* ends with an anticlimactic recognition that "total mediation" is impossible.[22] Yet, instead of giving up on the idea altogether, Ricoeur

20 Ibid., 257.
21 Ibid., 206.
22 Ibid., 207.

posits the collective singular, not as the oneness of time, but as "a limit-idea that is at the same time a regulative one."[23] Narrating historical time, then, becomes a Sisyphean task, but one that according to Ricoeur is nevertheless worthwhile. This is hardly a satisfying conclusion, however.

If attaining the summit of the collective singular view is impossible, is not our only recourse to hope that the boulder of narrative will roll down into a fertile valley? Surely the benefit of the narrative conception of temporality is that it permits one to see how time is used as a political category, and to understand why there are multiple temporalities. As I have already stated in the introduction, we know that different societies around the globe and throughout history have had several ways of orienting themselves in time. Even in the West, there have been significant changes in the conceptions of time over the centuries, as historians like Koselleck have argued. The multiplicity of temporalities is an observable cultural phenomenon. Of course, whether this multiplicity is preferable—from an ethical, political, and even existential perspective—to the impossible quest to reach for a collective singular historicity is another question. Ricoeur seems to think that it is not, and that a singular historical time is of clear value. But why not simply give up on the idea that historical time should take humanity as a whole as its subject?[24] Ricoeur's argument for the universal view is, in any case, rooted in what I think is problematic reasoning: "I hold that every expectation must be a hope for humanity as a whole, that humanity is not one species except insofar as it has one history, and that for there to be such a history, humanity as a whole must be its subject as collective singular."[25] Is this not a non sequitur that makes an unwarranted jump from genetics to narration? Humanity may become a central subject through narration, but it is one species as a matter of biological fact.

While some narratives are grander and some are more modest, all are necessarily selective, local, and particular. To insist that one

23 Ibid., 258.

24 The advantages of multiple temporalities is a topic that has already been explored. See, for example, Berber Bevernage, "Tales of Pastness and Contemporaneity: On the Politics of Time in History and Anthropology," *Rethinking History* 20, no. 3 (2016): 352–74; Helge Jordheim, "Against Periodization: Koselleck's Theory of Multiple Temporalities," *History and Theory* 51 (2012): 151–71.

25 Ricoeur, *Time and Narrative*, vol. 3, 215.

narrative is a collective singular time is to introduce a dubious hierarchy into the various levels of narrative temporality. And to say that one's narrative approaches a collective singular view is to assert that it is more objective—it is a more total view "from nowhere." The claim to the collective singular view is a claim to a God's-eye view, without direct mention of God. Ricoeur knew, of course, that philosophers of history who have focused on the centrality of narrativity in historical writing have already made this point. Louis Mink, for example, describes how the secularization of universal history involved the concealment of the author:

> [Universal History] was the claim that the ensemble of human events belongs to a single story. Yet there is no implication about who devises or tells the story. In its original theological form, as with Augustine, Universal History was the work of Divine Providence; but as the idea became secularized by the eighteenth century, God the Author retreated, leaving the idea of a story which is simply there, devised by no one . . . but waiting to be told by someone.[26]

But this is an effect of the narrative strategy, what Roland Barthes called the "referential illusion" of history writing which pretends "to allow the referent to speak all on its own."[27]

26 Louis Mink, "Narrative Form as a Cognitive Instrument," in R. H. Canary and H. Kozicki, eds., *The Writing of History: Literary Form and Historical Understanding* (Madison: University of Wisconsin Press, 1978, 129–49); and Louis Mink, *Historical Understanding* (Ithaca, NY: Cornell University Press, 1987), 190. Mink argues that "while objectivity is conceivable for a cumulative chronicle, it cannot really be translated into terms of narrative history (and in general the belief in historical objectivity fails to distinguish between narrative and chronicle, which has no form other than that of chronology and no relations among events other than temporal relations). A narrative must have a unity of its own; this is what is acknowledged in saying that it must have a beginning, middle and an end. And the reason why two narratives cannot be merely additively combined—in the simplest case by making them temporally continuous as the parallel chronicle is continuous—is that in the earlier narrative of such an aggregate the end is no longer an end, and therefore the beginning is no longer that beginning, nor the middle that middle. The more comprehensive narrative may be given its more formal unity, but this is a new unity, which replaces the independent coherence of each of its parts rather than uniting them." Ibid., 197.

27 Roland Barthes, "The Discourse of History," trans. Stephen Bann, *Comparative Criticism* 3 (1981): 7–20.

The question of who speaks the historical narrative is a crucial one, but Ricoeur's account leaves the answer ambiguous. Who narrates historical time? This is not so much a philosophical question as it is a sociological one. While it may be the case that all humans possess the capacity to configure historical narratives, it should be an obvious point that not all narratives have the same effectiveness, extent of reach, impact, or social role. On the contrary, in contemporary societies there are privileged authors, and the production, distribution, and consumption of historical narratives are conditioned to a large degree by economic and social factors and have physical limits. Moreover, the reflective instruments that Ricoeur claims are essential components in all narrations of historical time—clocks, calendars, the notion of generations, and so on—have been disseminated by political, religious, and economic institutions. As I have explained, the link between instruments of temporality and institutions of authority has been clearly documented.

In the modern era, nations with or without states have been some of the main promotors of historical narratives. Indeed, Ricoeur's call to view oneself in relation to a "historical community" reminds one of Johann Gottlieb Fichte's *Addresses to the German Nation* of 1808. A glance backward at the history of academic historical writing would suggest that what Ricoeur calls the historical community has usually been the nation.[28] Benedict Anderson, meanwhile, has explained how the calendar, the clock, and the newspaper facilitated a new conception of "simultaneity" that made it possible to imagine oneself as part of a contemporaneous national community at a singular historical moment.[29] In other words, it appears as if Ricoeur's philosophical anthropology assumes that we are all citizens of a modern nation-state with an unproblematic relations to a given "historical community." But what would his hermeneutics of historical consciousness have revealed

28 The links between professional historiography—as in research universities and the collection of testimony and traces in official archives—and nation-building are well known and were discussed in the introduction. For more detailed explorations of the connection between historiography and nationalism, see Stefan Berger and Christoph Conrad, *The Past as History: National Identity and Historical Consciousness in Modern Europe* (New York: Palgrave Macmillan, 2015); Berger Stefan and Chris Lorenz, eds., *Nationalizing the Past: Historians as Nation Builders in Modern Europe* (New York: Palgrave Macmillan, 2010).

29 Benedict Anderson, *Imagined Communities: Reflections on the Origin and Spread of Nationalism*, rev. ed. (London: Verso, 2016), 25–6.

if his implicit subject had been someone upon whom natal alienation and social death had been imposed?[30]

To be sure, there is no reason that nation-states should hold a monopoly on the narration of universal time. It is always possible to contest such narratives. In the age of globalization and neoliberalism, non-national or transnational historical narratives also exist.[31] Subaltern histories proliferate but rarely succeed in penetrating a public sphere that is so conditioned by the imperatives of commodity production.

Who narrates historical time in any given society? More often than not, the answer is someone else. If taken seriously, this admittedly somewhat flippant observation sheds new light on Ricoeur's category of the historical present. The historical present is not simply an activity in which individuals view their own lives from the historical perspective of a story about a historical community. Instead, they are called upon to view their lives from the perspective of a preexisting narrative that has been articulated by someone else; often someone in a position of power or who articulates a point of view congruent with the interests of the powerful. These privileged authors *interpellate* individuals as historical subjects when they inscribe their lives into the story of the historical community that is also constituted as a central subject through the same act. In this sense, the historical present is not only a political category, it is an ideological one. These narratives are, of course, presented "as the common interest of all the members of society" as Marx would say, even though, upon closer inspection, they usually correspond to recognizable political groups and class interests.[32]

An investigation that poses the question of who narrates historical time in a given society would likely show that it is often configured by interested groups and has the effect of *regulating* lived phenomenological time. In such cases, the effect of presenting the historical present as if the narrative were telling itself all on its own—as if it were

30 These concepts are drawn from Orlando Patterson's famous analysis of slavery in his *Slavery and Social Death: A Comparative Study* (Cambridge, MA: Harvard University Press, 2018).

31 Countervailing historiographical movements like world or global history are important in this regard. But historians writing under these labels regularly acknowledge that they can never achieve a total view.

32 Karl Marx and Friedrich Engels, *The German Ideology*, Marx-Engels Archive, marxists.org.

a collective singular view from nowhere—serves a double purpose: First, it conceals the point of view behind the particular narration. And, second, by presenting this narrative as a higher order level of time, it asserts the hermeneutic superiority of its perspective. The historical present becomes an injunction to self-periodization—that is to say, it is a call to view oneself in a historical context, where the modifier "historical" is intended to connote that the context is more real, or more complete in some way. In other words, one is called to read one's life as an exemplar or epiphenomenon of the time to which it belongs. The trials and tribulations of individual lives are rendered as details of a larger and more significant story. When individuals are interpellated by historical presents that have been preconfigured in this way, the evaluation of tradition that Ricoeur describes can become a command to respect existing institutions of domination. The "promise" he believes to be an essential part of the composite activity of the historical present becomes a commitment to fall into line with the imperatives of the historical community as that has been defined by someone else.

This is ideological in multiple senses of the term. When Ricoeur delivered a series of lectures on the topics of ideology and utopia shortly after publishing *Time and Narrative*, he identified three levels on which ideology operates: the levels of distortion (Marx's perspective), of legitimation (as in the Weberian view), and finally of integration and identity (as described by Clifford Geertz). On the most fundamental level, ideology plays a role in influencing praxis in the already-symbolic world in which humans exist. Events and actions must always take place against a background of social and cultural imagination. This symbolic dimension can be distorted and manipulated in order to narrow the gap between government and its legitimacy.[33]

Narratives of the historical present function on all three of these levels. Privileged authors seek to legitimize authority by presenting a particular story as the collective-singular interest of society in general. Through the referential illusion, the historical present distorts—turns on its head—the relationship between historical time and the individual: The historical narrative is thus transformed from a story articulated

33 Paul Ricoeur, *Lectures on Ideology and Utopia*, ed. George Howard Taylor (New York: Columbia University Press, 1986).

by an individual or group into an apparently autonomous agent—the historical process—to whose imperatives we must reconcile ourselves. Finally, historical presents are ideological in the Geertzian sense because they configure a world of already-symbolic action in such a way as to produce a refiguration of the lived experience of the individual. The problems one faces in daily life, seen in the context of the large story, appear insignificant or justified in pursuit of a larger goal or in the process of a broader evolution.

The ideological aspects of historical narration have been a central topic of concern for philosophers of history over the past decades. One of the main thinkers involved in this turn to the consideration of the use of figurative strategies and narration in scholarly historical writing has been Hayden White. White and Ricoeur commented extensively on each others' work even if, as David Pellauer has noted, the interaction between the two thinkers was less fruitful than it could have been considering their shared interests.[34] One of White's central claims was that the choice to prefigure what he called the "congeries of the historical field" in a particular way, and to choose a particular mode of emplotment, reflects not only a human impulse to moralize reality but the ideological commitments of the historian.[35] The historical present also reflects that same impulse.

Jacques Rancière comes close to my argument here when he applies his concept of the "distribution of the sensible," *le partage du sensible*, to temporality. A key term in Rancière's political philosophy, "distribution of the sensible" is defined as a particular definition of the world we share with others. It fixes an authoritative meaning on the common.[36]

34 David Pellauer, *Ricoeur and White on the Historical Imagination*, International Conference on Ricoeur Studies, University of Salento, Lecce, Italy, September 28, 2012, academia.edu.

35 He makes this argument in numerous places including Hayden White, "The Value of Narrativity in the Representation of Reality," in *The Content of the Form: Narrative Discourse and Historical Representation* (Baltimore: Johns Hopkins University Press, 1987), 21; and "Interpretation in History," *New Literary History* 4, no. 2 (1973): 281–314.

36 Rancière links his key term "police" with his other key phrase the "distribution of the sensible": "Politics is specifically opposed to the police. The police is a 'partition of the sensible' [*le partage du sensible*] whose principle is the absence of a void and of a supplement." Jacques Rancière, "Ten Theses on Politics," *Theory and Event* 5, no. 3 (2001).

Rancière explains that "to explicate a phenomenon by referring to 'its time' means to put into play a metaphysical principle of authority camouflaged as a methodological precept of historical inquiry."[37] In his 2011 lecture entitled *In What Time Do We Live?*, the term "historical present" does not appear. Instead, he reflects upon what is at stake when we make claims about the "state of things." By this he means statements of the kind I discussed at the start of this chapter; that is, claims about the nature of the present historical moment in which we are said to be living:

> A "state of things" includes the selection of a number of phenomena that are said to be characteristic of our present, the use of an interpretive frame within which they take on their significance, and the determination of a set of possibilities and impossibilities that derive from that given and its interpretation. In that sense, a "state of things" is a form of what I have proposed to call a distribution of the sensible: a set of relations between the perceptible, the thinkable, and the doable that defines a common world, defining thereby the way in which, and the extent to which, this or that class of human beings takes part in that common world.[38]

What Ricoeur calls historical presents are claims about the "state of things"; they are distributions of the sensible. When historical presents are articulated by privileged authors and enforced or acted upon by institutions, we could say, with Rancière, that they work to "order bodies" and allocate "ways of doing, ways of being, and ways of saying." By appealing to the authority of history—understood as a collective singular—they assert a hermeneutic superiority which can be used to determine what "speech is understood as discourse" or as simple "noise."[39] Historical

37 "A Conversation with Jacques Rancière," *Diacritics* 30, no. 2 (2000), 122. In another essay, Rancière expresses a similar point: "History is not simply a discipline; it is a mode of thought that, at a given moment, imposes a dominant sense of historicity as the general framework for understanding objects. The dominance of history is the dominance of a certain sense of history." Rancière, "Les mots de l'histoire du cinéma," *Les Cahiers du Cinéma* 496 (1995): 52 (my translation).

38 Jacques Rancière, "In What Time Do We Live?," *Política Común* 4 (2013).

39 Rancière defines the terms "police order" and "politics" as follows: "Politics is generally seen as the set of procedures whereby the aggregation and consent of collectives is achieved, the organization of powers, the distribution of places and roles, and the systems for legitimizing this distribution. I propose to give this system of distribution

presents that function in this way become what Rancière would call a "police order."

The hermeneutics of racism

Debates about reparations for slavery are clearly connected to the broader issue of the problem of "race" and racism. In the United States today, discussions of these topics often involve conflicts about the definition of the historical present. There are several competing narratives of the current historical moment; which is to say, that there are several views on how the question of racism should be considered in historical context. Here, I will focus on three in particular, which I will call the post-racial, the liberal, and the nationalist. All three are historical presents along the lines described by Ricoeur, which take a stance on tradition, and make a promise for the future. They seek to interpellate others as historical subjects. And while the first two can be called dominant, the third is subaltern. The dominance of the first two is rooted in the political and economic conditions that have governed their production, distribution, and consumption; they represent interests of powerful groups.

The idea that the present moment is a post-racial era was always a dubious proposition, but its absurdity became undeniably apparent during the first presidency of Donald Trump. It is easy to forget that many people sincerely believed in it—or, at least, took it seriously—during the period immediately prior to Barack Obama's election.[40] The post-racial narrative implied that racism in the United States was a problem that has been—or was in the process of being—historically transcended. Its message was clear: Racism was a real evil, to be sure, but it belongs to the now distant space of experience and is receding ever further from view. The Civil Rights Movement was the decisive turning point in this story, as it solved the problem of legal

---

and legitimization another name. I propose to call it *the police*." Jacques Rancière, *Disagreement: Politics and Philosophy* (Minneapolis: University of Minnesota Press, 2004), 28.

40 At the time, I wrote a more extensive analysis of post-racial discourse in Kenan Van de Mieroop, "On the Advantages and Disadvantages of Black History Month for Life: The Creation of the Post-Racial Era," *History and Theory* 55, no. 1 (2016): 3–24.

discrimination, and "we" are currently in a society in which race is becoming less significant. This is precisely the idea that, according to Dinesh D'Souza, most "white" Americans hold, as shown in the citation at the start of this chapter, from his 1995 book *The End of Racism*. The proper stance to take on tradition, in this case, is simply to forget, and not speak of or dwell upon the history of racism. The "promise" one must make to the historical community—which, in this narrative, is quite obviously the American nation—is to commit to ignoring "race" or adopting what is sometimes referred to as a color-blind approach. Even if this narrative has lost much of its initial persuasiveness (however limited), commentators on the right wing of the political spectrum in the United States still regularly describe racism as a historical phenomenon of declining significance, as exemplified in the recent tirades against critical race theory. In the minds of so many American conservatives it is the theory, not the racist acts that the theory attempts to grapple with, that is guilty of perpetuating racism and postponing the moment of its historical transcendence.

When it comes to understanding racism, the narrative of the mainstream liberal left in the United States has shifted considerably since the days of Obama. He articulated a vision of a nation that was still beset by problems of racism but was on course to overcoming them. According to that account, while the country was not yet in a post-racial era as conservatives claimed, it was on the horizon.[41] His "race speech" of 2008 was the most eloquent and famous articulation of the idea that America is a nation that, while marked by an "original sin" of slavery, is well on the way to getting past the problem of racism through a predestined, yet circuitous, process of national *Bildung*. The Civil War and the Civil Rights Movement were major turning points, but the brilliance of his speech was to position his own election as the climactic moment in the story. It was a call to patriotic action: Racism can be overcome by making use of the political structures of the American state to elect him as president.

41 See Ibid. Michael Tesler and David O. Sears have written about the complex ways in which the issue of "race" permeated the election campaign: Michael Tesler and David O. Sears, *Obama's Race: The 2008 Election and the Dream of a Post-Racial America* (Chicago: University of Chicago Press, 2010).

Since Trump's first election, however, the narrative of American racism articulated by mainstream liberals in the United States became far less optimistic. The post-racial horizon is remote. They now speak of racism as a clear and very present danger in the United States, and the forces of reaction, incarnated in Donald Trump, as determined to turn back the clock. His victory in 2016, which came as such a surprise to many, was seen to indicate how deeply rooted racism is in American society. A resurgence of bigotry left over from a previous era. What is needed now, some say, is a "racial reckoning" or national "atonement."[42] The political battle is construed increasingly in theological terms as one in which the soul of America is at stake.[43] Perhaps for this reason, many have subscribed to the call of the *New York Times*' 1619 Project, which has the express aim of giving slavery a central place in the American national narrative. The project's goal is "try[ing] to force us to acknowledge the truth about who we are so that we can try to build the country that we believe that we are."[44] Many of the leading candidates for the Democratic nomination for the presidency in 2019 supported the idea of reparations for slavery—at least rhetorically—in some form. This was quite a turnaround, because, in 2008, when Obama first ran for president, many commentators considered the idea marginal and outlandish.[45] Now, in the wake of Trump's reelection in 2024, it is not clear how the Democratic rhetoric will go forward, as many in the party appear to blame Kamala Harris's defeat on the supposed left-wing excesses of her campaign.

Both the post-racial and liberal narratives take the American nation as their central subject. This is not surprising, since they are so often articulated by political actors who seek to claim a role in the organs of

42 For example, an article by the Brookings Institution—a Democratic-leaning think tank—notes that in 2021 "the United States is again at a crossroads of racial reckoning." Ashley V. Reichelmann and Matthew O. Hunt, "How We Repair It: White American's Attitudes Toward Reparations," Brookings, December 8, 2021, brookings .edu.

43 I will explore the unmistakable Christian overtones that are present in this rhetoric in more detail in the next chapter.

44 Arun Venugopal, "'1619 Project' Journalist Says Black People Shouldn't Be an Asterisk in U.S. History," NPR, November 17, 2021, npr.org.

45 Jeff Stein, "Three 2020 Democrats Say 'Yes' to Race-Based Reparations—but Remain Vague on Details," *Washington Post*, February 22, 2019, washingtonpost .com.

the American state. They also both posit racism as a problem that has been or can be historically surpassed. Versions of these accounts reverberate in popular cultural and political discussions. Whether or not people agree with them, they are at least recognized as perspectives on the current situation that are often expressed. This is far less so when it comes to the final case that I wish to consider here, which I call the nationalist narrative. One version of it is short enough to reproduce in full:

> WHY ARE AFRICAN DESCENDANTS ENTITLED TO REPARATIONS?
> The Trans-Atlantic Slave "Trade" and chattel slavery, more appropriately called the Holocaust of Enslavement or Maafa/Maangamizi was and is a crime against humanity. Millions of Africans were brutalized, murdered, raped and tortured. They were torn from their families in Africa, kidnapped and lost family and community associations. African peoples in the United States and the prior colonies were denied the right to maintain their language, spiritual practices and normal family relations, always under the threat of being torn from newly created families at the whim of the "slave owner." Chattel slavery lasted officially from 1619 to 1865. It was followed by 100 years of government led and supported denial of equal and humane treatment including Black Codes, convict lease, sharecropping, peonage, and Jim Crow practices of separate and unequal accommodations. African descendants continue to be denied rights of self-determination, inheritance, and full participation in the United States government and society. The laws and practices in the United States continue to treat African peoples in a manner similar to slavery—maintaining dual systems in virtually every area of life including punishment, health care, education and wealth, maintaining the myths of White superiority and African and African descendants' inferiority.[46]

The central subject of the nationalist narrative is "African descendants" or "African peoples" not "generations of Americans."

46 National Coalition of Blacks for Reparations in America (N'COBRA) website, ncobra.org.

Obama's speech offered an "integrationist" vision; N'COBRA's, quoted above, a separatist one. Self-determination is one of their key political demands. The different periodizations—the different beginnings, middles, and ends—of the two narratives underscores these positions: Obama's narrative starts with the foundation and the Constitutional Convention (1787), while N'COBRA's account begins in 1619, the date that the first enslaved Africans arrived to the Virginia Colony and therefore connects "African descendants" in America more explicitly with the African continent. If Obama's account was, in the terms of narrative theory, emploted as a romance (understood as a story of liberation, self-fulfillment, and victory of good over evil), N'COBRA's account may be best described as a tragedy. Obama construed America as a heroic nation progressing through history by the actions of generations of virtuous citizens, while N'COBRA recounts the eternal return of the repression of "African descendants" in order to make a case for their self-determination.

All three narratives serve to contextualize the current historical moment in light of past events and visions of the future. They present very different frameworks through which to interpret instances of current-day racism. We can see this in the hermeneutic conflicts that have arisen around the widely debated police killings in the US. From the perspective of the post-racial era, it is anachronistic to view these shootings as racist. Consequently, those who assert that a police officer was motivated by racism are themselves guilty of importing racist concepts into the present, where they do not belong. It is they who are keeping racism alive, and it is they who insist on clinging to the past. Calls for slavery reparations are, likewise, seen as an example of this refusal to let go. The liberal narrative, on the other hand, does recognize police shootings as racist incidents; they are so much about "race" that according to some critics they ignore class-based analyses of police violence.[47] The narrative furthermore suggests that these are indications that "we still have a long way to go," implying that it will take more time to solve the problem of racism. The teleology however

47 This criticism has been made by a number of writers, notably Adolph Reed Jr., who speaks of a "race-reductionism." See Adolph Reed Jr., "Why Black Lives Matter Can't Be Co-opted," *nonsite.org*, July 23, 2021; Hope Reese, "Adolph Reed, Jr.: The Perils of Race Reductionism," *JSTOR Daily*, April 28, 2021, daily.jstor.org.

remains clear: A utopian moment during which America fulfills its promise is on the horizon, even if it is far more remote than it seemed in 2008. But the rise of Trump threatens the whole project of American democracy, and racist incidents are manifestation of this spiritual conflict and proof that racist reactionaries are determined to hold back progress.

From the perspective of the nationalist N'COBRA narrative, the police shootings are simply another manifestation of the same old story. They are not events on a crossroad; they are examples of a persistent racist structure which cannot be historically transcended but must be decisively broken with. That break can only be achieved by starting a new society on totally different premises. In this view, reparations are not a way to achieve reconciliation and let America fulfill its destiny; instead, they are a policy that would be part of a broader project of national self-determination.

To state that these three contesting narratives constitute different presents—presents that are full of political significance, that portray symbolic actions in a particular light, and that seek to commit individuals to political projects—is not to state that they are equal. Powerful groups disseminate the first two narratives. D'Souza's book *The End of Racism* was distributed by the neoconservative Free Press, which also produced *The Bell Curve*, *Illiberal Education*, and *The Tempting of America*. The Heritage Foundation—a think tank with several millions of dollars at its disposal—actively promoted these works. Obama, for his part, could rely on the power of national television to transmit his narrative. In contrast, N'COBRA's narrative, without powerful groups or institutions to back it, has had limited influence and reach. The material circumstances of its production, distribution, and consumption are completely different.

Yet all these narratives of the historical present can be called ideological in that they interpellate subjects as historical—in the first two cases, as "American citizens" and, in the third, as "African descendants"—and have different implications for political action. In the first case, to adopt color-blindism or do nothing. The second narrative is formulated as a quasi-secularized prophetic call to return to the righteous path of American liberty from which we have strayed, by engaging in patriotic antiracism and atoning for the "original sin" of slavery, all while voting out the forces of Trumpian reaction.[48] In the third case, the political message is not about the saving or condemning the reputation of the West or America, it is plainly a call to fight for national self-determination.[49]

48 Here, I use the term "prophetic" in relationship to history following the analysis of Jayne Svenungsson, who explains that "the fact that God holds sway over history means that the future, far from being laid out in advance, is conditional upon choices made in the present moment by God's people. The prophets' preoccupation with the future must be understood in this context—not as the augury of a predetermined future but as an exhortation to the people to choose the path of God in the present and thereby create a different future. When proclaiming redemption the prophets have in mind repentance—in Hebrew, *teshuvah*—literally, a 'return' to the path marked out by God." Jayne Svenungsson, *Divining History: Prophetism, Messianism, and the Development of the Spirit* (New York: Berghahn Books, 2016), 15.

49 It is interesting to note how these positions are congruent with the typology of utopias in the work of Karl Mannheim (to whom Ricoeur refers in *Ideology and Utopia*): For conservatives utopia is already here; for liberals, it is in the future; and for radicals, it is imminent if only a revolution can take place. Ricoeur, *Lectures on Ideology and Utopia*, 274.

3

Inheriting Debt, Sin, and the Curse of Ham

Political responsibility . . . exists quite apart from what the individual member of the group has done and therefore can neither be judged on moral terms nor be brought before a criminal court . . . It means hardly more, generally speaking than that every generation, by virtue of being born into a historical continuum, is burdened by the sins of the fathers as it is blessed by the deeds of the ancestors.
—Hanna Arendt, in Iris Marion Young, *Responsibility for Justice*

Intergenerational Justice

During a trip to Dakar in the summer of 2007, Nicolas Sarkozy addressed "all Africans" in a speech that was full of remarks which irked many in his intended audience; most memorable, perhaps, was the French President's pontification that "no one can ask sons to repent for the mistakes of their fathers."[1] Everyone present understood this to be a reference to the issue of reparations for slavery and colonialism. In making that statement Sarkozy repeated what might be the most common objection to reparations claims. The message was clear: Africa

1 Nicolas Sarkozy, "L'Intégralité du discours de Dakar prononcé par Nicolas Sarkozy," *Le Nouvel Obs*, July 27, 2007, nouvelobs.com (my translation).

and France should let bygones be bygones. Africans should forget the past of slavery and colonialism and move on.[2]

Earlier in the same year, at home in France, Sarkozy had recently won election on a campaign platform that promised, among other things, to reinvigorate the concept of "national identity" in French political culture. Once in power, he created a new ministry for immigration and national identity in an effort to make good on this promise. The concept of national identity he espoused involved an attitude toward history that was almost the opposite of the one he urged Africans adopt: It demanded the recollection and glorification of the great episodes of the nation's past. Later, in his role as leader of Les Républicains, Sarkozy would explain that his view of national identity required one to embrace one's historical origins, and take up responsibility for what has been inherited from previous generations: "The identity of France is, first of all, the landscapes fashioned by almost 100 generations who patiently cleared, ploughed and sowed this land to which we are, often negligent, heirs today."[3] No one noticed that the cutting of sugarcane was omitted from his list of arduous agricultural tasks.

An ambiguity is apparent in Sarkozy's comments on intergenerational relations. On the one hand, he declared that people today cannot be held responsible for mistakes of the past, as if stating an elementary moral principle. On the other hand, he articulated the view that current generations are deeply indebted to their ancestors for everything that they have inherited, as if this were equally a matter of common sense. These two views of how contemporaries should relate to their past appear, at the very least, to be in tension with one another. But is this tension a contradiction? Some might argue that it is perfectly consistent to recognize that we are heirs to previous generations while simultaneously rejecting the claim that we are responsible for their mistakes. Others could respond that it is opportunistic to pick and choose what we want to inherit from

2 This speech provoked a great deal of critical response. See, for example, the essays in Makhily Gassama, ed., *L'Afrique répond à Sarkozy: Contre le discours de Dakar* (Paris: Philippe Rey, 2013).

3 Discours de Nicolas Sarkozy, Président des Républicains, au Colloque du Think Tank France Fière – Identité(s) française, entre fierté et désamour, May 24, 2016 (my translation). Nicolas Lemasne, "Nicolas Sarkozy rejoue l'ode à l'identité nationale," *Le Monde*, May 25, 2016, lemonde.fr. The full text of the speech is available on Sarkozy's Facebook page as "L'identité de la France."

the past and that if we are going to recognize the good things we have received from posterity, then we must accept responsibility for the bad things as well. Both positions appear reasonable.

A number of philosophers writing in the tradition of liberal political thought have spilled a considerable amount of ink attempting to articulate theories of justice that resolve this tension. These thinkers sometimes use the case of reparations for slavery as an exemplum for a new normative theory of justice across generations. In this literature, the call for slavery reparations is treated as one example of a movement for historical justice alongside several others—reparation and commemoration of the Holocaust and other genocides among the most notable. The task that they set themselves is to develop an account of intergenerational justice that would cover all these cases and potentially several more. Their discussions have sometimes been extended toward a consideration of future generations and the ethical dilemmas involved in the transmission of environmental debt and the risks of climate change to them. It is not clear, however, that a similar notion of intergenerational justice will suffice to cover both temporal directions: While it is obvious that actions we undertake in the present will have effects into the future, it is far from obvious that we have any moral obligation to generations long dead.[4]

Although there certainly are philosophers who advocate a view in which contemporaries have a moral duty toward the dead, several notable contemporary scholars reject the idea that current generations can be held culpable for past crimes and instead seek to found a theory of historical justice on the basis of a distinction between guilt and responsibility.[5] On this view, current generations are certainly not guilty of

4 The philosophical literature on intergenerational justice is extensive. Some important volumes include Stephen M. Gardiner, ed., *The Oxford Handbook of Intergenerational Ethics* (Oxford: Oxford University Press, 2021); Axel Gosseries and Lukas Meyer, eds., *Intergenerational Justice* (Oxford: Oxford University Press, 2012). Also see Lukas Meyer, "Intergenerational Justice," in Edward N. Zalta, ed., *The Stanford Encyclopedia of Philosophy*, Summer 2021 ed., plato.stanford.edu.

5 Philosophers who argue for moral responsibility to the past include: Jeffery Blustein, *The Moral Demands of Memory* (Cambridge: Cambridge University Press, 2012); Anton Froeyman, *History, Ethics, and the Recognition of the Other: A Levinasian View on the Writing of History* (New York: Routledge, 2019); and to a lesser extent Paul Ricoeur, *Memory, History, Forgetting*, trans. Kathleen Blamey and David Pellauer (Chicago: University of Chicago Press, 2010).

historical crimes but they still do have a moral responsibility to repair them. In what is perhaps the most influential version of this argument, Iris Marion Young suggests that we should move away from the "liability model" in favor of a "social connection model." In a similar vein, Janna Thompson has argued against the "legalist" paradigm that has dominated discussions on historical injustice. Instead, she maintains that we should take responsibility for the past.[6] She sees this responsibility as a duty to be embraced, as opposed to a question of culpability. Both Young and Thompson recommend a substitution of the adversarial language of guilt and debt with terms such as "responsibility" and "solidarity," which might also be more palatable to contemporary citizens who are the beneficiaries of past injustices.

Young, in particular, presents compelling arguments that function well as normative theories to tackle the question of how societies should deal with historical injustices in general and in an ideal situation. But the applicability of these arguments to the cases she uses as examples—German guilt after World War II and slavery reparations—misses something fundamental concerning the historical circumstances in which said claims arose. First, the legalist paradigm in reparations discourse and the language of guilt, debt, and culpability that it uses—and which she rejects—is primarily a reflection of the fact that reparations claims have by necessity been made in courts, and as such have been forced to use legal vocabulary. Turning to the courts was a tactic, as opposed to an end in itself. It was employed precisely because broader society has demonstrated a lack of political commitment to extending any notion of social connection to populations that have been segregated on the basis of ethnoracial classifications, and who, because of historical circumstances that preceded their births sometimes by centuries, have inherited a marginal social-economic and political status.

Second, Young, in particular, does not take into consideration that the moral obligation to atone for the sins of predecessors and the inheritance of guilt have an extremely long and venerable lineage in moral and political thought in the so-called West and Middle East. She seems

6 Klaus Neumann and Janna Thompson, "Introduction: Beyond the Legalist Paradigm," in *Historical Justice and Memory* (Madison: University of Wisconsin Press, 2015); Janna Thompson, *Taking Responsibility for the Past: Reparation and Historical Injustice* (Malden, MA: Polity, 2002).

to suggest that those who demand that historic injustices be rectified in the present are putting forward new, inchoate moral theories about how current generations ought to relate to the past. In fact, these groups are merely appealing to preexisting and well-established ideas that have been considered normal and acceptable in other instances.

Consider her comments on Arendt's claim in *Eichmann in Jerusalem* that:

> political responsibility . . . exists quite apart from what the individual member of the group has done and therefore can neither be judged on moral terms nor be brought before a criminal court . . . It means hardly more, generally speaking than that every generation, by virtue of being born into a historical continuum, is burdened by the sins of the fathers as it is blessed by the deeds of the ancestors.

Young criticizes this argument, stating that

> This cannot be all there is to political responsibility. It is plausible to say that "being born into a historical continuum" loads onto every person the imperative to take an attitude toward, and often to take specific action in relation to wrongs committed by one's political ancestors. Leaving aside the difficulties in determining just who counts as the "fathers" for particular people, this cannot be all there is to political responsibility . . . In "Collective Responsibility" as well as in "Organized Guilt," Arendt suggests that what it means to say that contemporaries share responsibility is that they are members of the same political community in whose name the crimes have been committed. This sounds almost neo-Platonist: just by virtue of my participation in the entity that is the nation, I bear responsibility. Interpreted thusly, this idea of responsibility seems similar to but less honest than the notion of "metaphysical guilt" that Karl Jaspers proposed and Arendt rejected.[7]

Young may be correct in finding the notion that one bears responsibility "just by virtue of my participation in the entity that is the nation" to be

7 Iris Marion Young, *Responsibility for Justice* (New York: Oxford University Press, 2011), 80.

preposterous and "neo-Platonist," but the idea is hardly Arendt's invention, nor does it come from Jaspers: It is simply a core aspect of thought in nationalism, a political idea which historians regard to be at least as important in the modern period as is liberalism, if not more so. This passage is consistent with Young's rejection of nationalism in favor of cosmopolitanism and, therefore, is a testament to the soundness of her normative approach. But this comes at the cost of diminishing the historical context in which such claims are made; a context in which the national political responsibility she dismisses is very often understood as the norm. And in Nazi Germany, the focus of Arendt's discussion, this idea was taken to an extreme. In both of Young's examples, the victims of historical crimes in fact made use of the dominant moral, political, and legal language of the age, they did not invent a new one. That was part of their rhetorical strategy.

I do not mean to say that Young is wrong to criticize the notion of inherited responsibility; it does appear to be problematic. Nevertheless, it is a view about intergenerational relations within nations that is commonly articulated and acted out or performed. It is an idea that long predates discussions of reparations for slavery. By all accounts, movements for reparations for historical injustices are comparatively new phenomena and are judged by scholars to be notable precisely because they were, until very recently, an unusual form of politics. If this is so, then it raises the question why these cases should be chosen as a battleground upon which to fight a broader philosophical struggle against the centuries-old notion of inherited guilt and responsibility across generations.

In this chapter, my intention is not to contribute to a normative moral and political philosophy of intergenerational responsibility. Instead, I lay out the competing notions of responsibility and obligation across generations, which, I will argue, have been influential and formative of political thought for centuries. The age-old idea that each new generation should not be held accountable for the actions of previous generations has always coexisted with the competing view in which obligations across time and between generations are stressed. In reviewing this history, one finds that many thinkers over the centuries have held seemingly contradictory and inconsistent views about the nature of intergenerational obligations. Sarkozy, in other words, is in good company.

"Ancestral fault"

The two predominant contrasting ideas regarding intergenerational relations can be found in the Hebrew Bible, although they are undoubtedly much older. Nevertheless, because of the widespread influence of the Abrahamic religions in the contemporary world, it is convenient to begin my account of these seemingly incongruent ideas, not at their point of origin but with a discussion of one of the most influential iterations of them.

When Nicolas Sarkozy spoke of the immorality of making sons repent for the sins of their ancestors, he echoed Ezekiel 18:20: "The soul that sinneth, it shall die. The son shall not bear the iniquity of the father, neither shall the father bear the iniquity of the son: the righteousness of the righteous shall be upon him, and the wickedness of the wicked shall be upon him."[8] But when Arendt wrote that each generation is burdened by the sins of their ancestors, she, too, referred to an ancient concept conveyed in the Bible, as in this passage from Exodus 20: 5–6:

> Thou shalt not bow down thyself to them, nor serve them: for I the Lord thy God am a jealous God, visiting the iniquity of the fathers upon the children unto the third and fourth generation of them that hate me; and showing mercy of thousands of them that love me, and keep my commandments.[9]

A similar idea appears in Numbers 14:18: "The lord is long-suffering and of great mercy, forgiving iniquity and transgression, and by no means clearing the guilty, visiting the iniquity of the fathers upon the children unto the third and fourth generation."[10] These two ideas of intergenerational relations appear to be in contradiction with one another. To be sure, believers of the Abrahamic religions and those more knowledgeable about these Scriptures than myself may argue that these notions can, in fact, be reconciled. Whether or not this is possible is a theological question. The questions that concern us here are how these

8 *The Bible: King James Version with the Apocrypha*, ed. David Norton (London: Penguin, 2006), 1105. In the Quran, the same idea is referred to in Surat An-najm, 53, 38–40; *The Koran*, trans. N. J. Dawood (London: Penguin, 2014), 526.

9 *The Bible*, 91.

10 Ibid., 185.

two notions were passed down in history and how they have influenced sublunary affairs. What is at issue in the reparations debates, after all, is not whether God will punish former slaveholders or the perpetrators of the Holocaust, but rather what humans in subsequent generations must (or should) undertake (or suffer) as a consequence of those actions.

If opponents of reparations invoke the moral maxim Sarkozy repeated in Dakar, they should, at the very least, be aware of the existence of the opposing principle with an equally ancient lineage, not only in the tradition of Jerusalem but also in the Athenian one. The classicist Renaud Gagné has named the second principle "ancestral fault." Far from being a marginal idea, he argues that it was a central notion in ancient Greek thought, and that it has been passed down from that time to become a "keystone of Western Culture." The following pages owe a great deal to Gagné's remarkable book *Ancestral Fault in Ancient Greece*, as I attempt to enter into a constructive and critical dialogue with his writing on this topic.

Gagné's first move is to reformulate the concept we are discussing into new terms. He uses the phrase "ancestral fault" because this is an emic category, a translation of the Greek term *progonikon hamartema*. He avoids the more common term "inherited guilt" that developed later and is loaded with Christian connotations and which he would like to put aside in order to focus on the appearance of the concept in the ancient world. Gagné is, of course, also interested in the reception of Greek thought and its reinterpretation in scholarship over subsequent centuries and thus devotes a great deal of his book to an exploration of that dynamic. Before he proceeds, however, he explains that ancestral fault was an idea whose importance should not be underestimated:

> This is a concept at the heart of ancient Greek thinking on theodicy, inheritance, privilege, and suffering, the links of wealth and morality, individual responsibility, the bonds that unite generations, and the grand movements of history. It played a major role in some of the most critical and pressing reflections of Greek culture on divinity, society and human knowledge.[11]

11 Renaud Gagné, *Ancestral Fault in Ancient Greece* (Cambridge: Cambridge University Press, 2016), 3.

It is for this reason that the concept plays a central role in *De decem dubitationibus circa providentiam*, written by Proclus (c. 410–485 CE), a key text which Gagné argues represents an attempt to resume Hellenic tradition in a coherent way. It is interesting to note, in connection with Young's objection to Arendt mentioned earlier, that this work was intended for students at the Neoplatonic school in Athens.[12] In his discussion of the ninth question, Proclus reflects on the idea that "although others have committed the crime, fathers for instance, or ancestors, justice falls upon their descendants."[13] Proclus presents a defense of this principle, which he views as a crucial part of the Hellenic worldview.[14] The logic of his argument rests upon an understanding that the city or a family is a single life form (*animal unum*) that is more important, in ways, than the single human life and that is "homochronous." There is, therefore, a temporal argument at the heart of his reasoning, in that ancestors and descendants are united in a common experience. As such, actions that are undertaken by the *animal unum* at earlier times produce effects later on. Proclus draws a striking parallel with the functioning of a disease: An illness may lie dormant and emerge at a later time or manifest itself elsewhere in the body.[15] Carrying on the medical analogy Proclus presents the intervention of Providence as a sort of medicinal or surgical treatment of the body of the *animal unum*:

> In the same way, then, Providence uncovers the defects that souls have in them and that come, through heredity, from the souls that have committed wrong before, and that is why, even if, although they have a similar nature, they have not done what their predecessors have done, still she punishes them, so as to preventively extirpate the evil, as if it were latent epilepsy. For, just as warts, black stains, and hereditary marks, while they are not visible in their children or grandchildren, can reappear in later descendants, particular characteristics of *ethos* can reappear in individuals who are quite distant from each other in time, characteristics unknown to all except the One, to whom it is given to know them and preventively destroy them. And what

12 Ibid., 23.
13 Proclus (58) cited ibid., 24.
14 Ibid.
15 Gagné, *Ancestral Fault*, 25–6.

> clearly demonstrates the presence of a similarity is the fact that they believe the punishments that they pay are the consequences of the faults of their ancestors.[16]

Gagné notes that the figure of the collective body and the metaphors of disease and medical intervention are not incidental but, in fact, often used in Greek texts about ancestral fault. He cites a scholion to Hesiod's *Works and Days*, which sees Proclus's idea of ancestral fault in a poem written around 700 BC.[17] This seems to illustrate a remarkable continuity in the language used to describe ancestral fault. The scholion says:

> Indeed, the faults of the fathers also defile their descendants and reveal them as bound to retribution. For blame and ill repute also come upon them from these wrongdoings, and, inheriting vengeance from the crimes that their fathers committed, they share in the punishments that are their due. Divinity knows, in any case, that something of the unjust inclination of their progenitors grows into their character, even if it escapes our attention, and seeing this rot in them, they justly cut it down for vengeance and so as not to let it grow, as doctors preventively purge some sickness which they suspect.[18]

The explanations of ancestral fault that Gagné presents may strike many a modern reader as—*pace* Young—being rather sensible. Of course, one may be left cold by the language of Providence and the notion of a single shared soul as well as by the frank talk of revenge as a justifiable motive. But the core idea that the "faults of the fathers also defile their descendants" seems sound as an observation of how grudges and feuds tend to persist and linger if they are not dealt with and resolved. This, of course, is not to suggest that the descendants are "guilty" or "deserving" of punishment in any moral sense. It appears that the Greeks saw the issue in different terms. They did not isolate moral transmission as a specific

16 Proclus cited ibid., 26.

17 On the origin of the scholion Gangé has the following to say: "The scholia to the *Works and Days* are largely based on the lost commentary of Proclus on the Hesiodic poem, and there can be no doubt that the scholion to verse 284 is, at least in part, a reflection of that commentary, and of Proclus' discussion of 'the injustices of the fathers' in it," *Ancestral Fault*, 30.

18 Ibid., 29.

type of heredity. Instead, they understood transmission between generations to take many interlinked forms: Character and reputation, genetic traits, responsibility, curses and blessings, wealth and poverty, could all be passed down to descendants.[19] There does not seem to be a strict separation of moral and material inheritance, for example; instead, these are interlinked. The final citation is not so much a justification of the idea of punishing descendants for the faults of their ancestors as it is an observation—difficult to deny—that misdeeds have impacts that last far beyond the lifetime of their original perpetrators. To expect—as some might want to—that such misdeeds will disappear beneath the sands of time is folly. It would be more apt to say that a wound inflicted at a certain period and left to fester is unlikely to heal without intervention. The endurance of the legacies of slavery and colonialism in contemporary societies appears to be a vindication of this ancient Greek wisdom.

We may readily accept the idea that an evil can linger for generations and that descendants may be blamed or held responsible for the misdeeds of their ancestors. We may also draw from this the conclusion that some intervention is necessary to "extirpate" a lingering evil, so as to avoid its perpetuation. Such ideas would not be out of place in a transitional justice handbook. The more difficult questions are who or what should be given the task of cutting out the rot and how that excision should actually be undertaken (or, indeed, whether a milder therapeutic approach should be used). It is one thing for Providence or the divine to punish descendants for ancestral fault, and it is quite another thing for humans to do so.

These dilemmas were reformulated in new terms when the idea of ancestral fault was passed down through the Christian tradition and reinterpreted through a biblical framework.[20] Gagné argues that the Christian reception of the Greek idea of ancestral fault was characterized by competing processes of "domestication," on the one hand, and "foreignization," on the other, and that this dialectic continued into the early modern and modern periods.[21] For some Christian thinkers,

19 Gagné notes how the transmission of wealth implied the transmission of responsibility, *Ancestral Fault*, 33.

20 Ibid., 63–4.

21 Ibid., 64.

> Greek ancestral fault continued to be perceived . . . as a direct counterpart to the corporate responsibility of the Old Testament, and the inherited stain of original sin. Read through the medieval and early modern theological tradition, it became indexed to the language of Christian programmes on Providence, responsibility, and sin.[22]

It was thus considered to be a divine principle which informed notions of justice in human law. But there was also an important tradition of thinkers who sought to reject this as a principle and deny its applicability to the contemporary world.[23] Yet even those who criticized the concept of ancestral fault understood that it was a vital idea that needed to be wrestled with. The Christian reception of the doctrine of ancestral fault was, in other words, marked by an ambiguity.

The curse of Ham, original sin, and its critics

Quite apart from any Greek influence, similar ideas about intergenerational transmission existed within the Abrahamic tradition, but these are beyond the scope of Gagné's account. One of the most important iterations of the notion of inherited guilt in (early) modern history was, undoubtedly, the idea of the Hamitic curse, which was regularly used as a justification for slavery. It is remarkable that well into the nineteenth century, apologists for slavery defended the institution on the basis of a reading of Genesis 9, in which Noah, who is angry with Ham, casts a curse on Ham's son, Canaan, and condemns him and his descendants to slavery.

Among the scholars who have written on the reception of the Hamitic curse and its use as a justification for slavery, the work of David M.

22 Ibid., 81.

23 Ibid. As influential representative thinkers in the former tradition, Gagné cites Willibald Pirckheimer (1470–1530), Daniel Wyttenbach (1746–1820), and the reactionary thinker Joseph de Maistre (1753–1821). Georges Méautis (1890–1970), a classicist who produced an edition of Plutarch's *De sera numinis vindicta* in 1935, compared the Greek idea of ancestral fault and the notion that the individual could be held responsible for the *polis* and the family, to the contemporary idea that a person is part of a "race" and a nation. The most notable representatives of the latter tradition of "foreignization" are, according to Gagné, Hugo Grotius and Jan Lomeier. We will consider the work of some of these thinkers below.

Goldenberg—especially his 2017 book *Black and Slave: The Origins and History of the Curse of Ham*—stands out for its breadth of examples and the time period it covers. He examines the use of the story of the Hamitic curse in Jewish, Christian, and Islamic traditions and explains how it migrated from the Middle East to Europe and the New World, and how it remained relevant into the twentieth century. He presents numerous startling examples of its iteration. Among them is an extract from an interview with Gus (Jabbo) Rogers that was part of the WPA Slave Narrative Collection, a project between 1936 and 1938. In it, Rogers explains that he had been condemned to slavery because of the Hamitic curse: "You just can't get away from what the Lord said."[24] This example illustrates the remarkable longevity of this rationalization of slavery. Goldenberg notes that the abundance of evocations and refutations of the Hamitic curse in the American sources during the nineteenth century demonstrate the persuasive power of this form of argument.[25] Abolitionists were obliged to spend a significant amount of time and energy refuting it. While his review of the abolitionist literature is far from exhaustive, it is nevertheless interesting to note that the preferred way of countering invocations of the curse of Ham was to dispute the assertion that the enslaved were the descendants of Canaan. Arguments suggesting that it might not be fair to punish descendants for the crimes committed by their ancestors or that after several millennia, it might be time to let bygones be bygones, are surprisingly rare among the examples presented. Goldenberg cites only one instance in which an abolitionist took issue with the notion that descendants should be held responsible for the faults of their ancestors. This was the case of the Quaker John Woolman (1720–1772), for whom the idea that guilt could be inherited was repugnant to "solid Principles."[26]

24 These interviews were part of the New Deal Federal Writers Project between 1936–1938. David M. Goldenberg, *Black and Slave: The Origins and History of the Curse of Ham* (Berlin: De Gruyter, 2017), 151.

25 Ibid., 148.

26 In an essay published in 1762 Woolman wrote: "To suppose it right that an innocent Man shall at this Day be excluded from the common Rules of Justice; be deprived of that Liberty which is the natural Right of human Creatures; and be a Slave to others during Life, on Account of a sin committed by his immediate Parents; or a Sin committed by Ham, the Son of Noah, is a Supposition too gross to be admitted into the mind of any Person, who Sincerely desires to be governed by solid Principles." Cited in *Black and Slave*, 148.

By contrast, during the same period and even earlier, the famous Christian tenet according to which all of humanity is born with inherited or original sin (*Erbsünde*) ever since Adam and Eve were expelled from the Garden of Eden was thrown into question. That doctrine played an important role in many branches of Christianity and was greatly influenced by Augustine's forceful rejection of the Pelagian interpretation of the meaning of the Genesis story.[27] Part of this dispute revolved around the issue of whether or not babies were born with sin inherited from Adam. According to the Pelagian interpretation, infants came into this world innocent, but for Augustine only the sacrament of baptism could remove the stain of sin.[28]

To be sure, there has been a great deal of discussion among Christians about the nature and meaning of original sin for centuries. But these debates became increasingly important during the Protestant Reformation and afterward.[29] A number of historians have argued that the qualification and refutation of the idea during the early modern period and the Enlightenment constituted a major turning point in the history of "Western thought."[30] Indeed, some have said that if a unifying theme can be found in all the various and diverse strands of Enlightenment thought, it is precisely the common rejection of the doctrine of inherited original sin. In its Augustinian interpretation, it carried an important message about human nature, and much of the scholarship that has analyzed the critiques of this idea by European

27 Matthew Kadane, "Original Sin and the Path to the Enlightenment," *Past and Present* 235 (2017), 105.

28 Alan Jacobs, *Original Sin: A Cultural History* (New York: HarperOne, 2008), 47, 50.

29 Alan Jacobs argues that "The protestant reformation did not bring about any substantially new teaching regarding original sin. The leading theologians of the movement, with the partial exception of the great Swiss reformer Ulrich Zwingli, forcefully reaffirmed the Augustinian teachings, which they believed had been diluted by medieval theologians" (ibid., 106). However, this reaffirmation of the Augustinian view took place at a time when "multiple cultural and social forces mounted increasingly strong resistance, if not (at first) to belief in original sin itself, then at least to its doctrinal and practical importance" (107). Of course, these ideas were not only being discussed by Protestants. Jacobs also discusses the debates among Catholic groups that were provoked by the work of Cornelius Jansen (109–10).

30 For example, Ernst Cassirer wrote: "The concept of original sin is the common opponent against which all the different trends of the philosophy of the Enlightenment join forces." Cited in Jacobs, *Original Sin*, 150.

thinkers in the seventeenth and eighteenth centuries has focused on that element of the story. But the idea of original sin also contained a message about the inheritance of guilt across generations. And while it was criticized on many grounds, it is notable, as we shall see, that some began to invoke what we might call a temporal argument in order to contest and even to ridicule the belief that descendants of Adam and Eve could be held accountable for sin, even after thousands of years had elapsed.

In one of the most interesting studies of the debates around original sin during this period, Michael Heyd argues that England witnessed a dramatic "transformation in the doctrine and experience of original sin," which constituted nothing less than one of the most profound changes of "*mentalité* in protestant Europe" and was a key turning point in the transition to the Enlightenment.[31] Different aspects of the doctrine had long been the subject of disagreement and dispute. Among the important issues in the debate were the state of the world before Adam and Eve's transgression, the causes and consequences of original sin, and, importantly for our purposes, the question of what exactly was transferred from Adam to his descendants (sin and guilt) and what constituted the punishment; "eternal mortality or just temporal mortality, women's labor at childbirth, man's labor in order to make a living."[32] Heyd suggests that the last two questions in particular became a source of controversy in late seventeenth-century England because of the different interpretations of original sin among Calvinists, Puritans, Arminians, and Catholics. These debates took on an extra level of urgency during the interregnum and the generations following it. There was a growing and widespread concern that individual moral responsibility needed to be emphasized and encouraged in the context of an unstable political situation.[33] The rise of antinomian tendencies and radical sects was perceived as a worrying development, and this, Heyd claims, made the reexamination of the idea of original sin an urgent task: "The Reformed idea of original sin—the notion that man had been

31 Michael Heyd, "Original Sin, the Struggle for Stability, and the Rise of Moral Individualism in Late Seventeenth-Century England," in Philip Benedict and Myron Gutmann, eds., *Early Modern Europe from Crisis to Stability* (Newark: University of Delaware Press, 2005), 197.

32 Ibid., 199.

33 Ibid., 210.

in any case guilty from birth, and that only divine grace could ensure the performance of good works—all threatened to lead men to passivity and to disregard moral norms."[34]

Heyd goes on to review the work of a number of influential English writers whose ideas, he suggests, would have been widely disseminated in sermons and catechisms.[35] His account of the way that the Calvinist interpretation of original sin was handed down and reinterpreted indicates that these debates paralleled the developing political theory of the day. Heyd tells us that Calvin followed Augustine in seeing humanity as a single "organism" and held the view that children were born with the sin inherited from Adam and were thus *guilty*. But this picture was immediately transformed by the subsequent generation of his followers who argued that sin could be inherited but that guilt was more properly understood as being "imputed." The account developed by Calvinists and Puritans sometimes called "federal theology" constituted what Heyd describes as a "legal" interpretation of original sin. On this view, Adam is presented as the "representative" of humanity as opposed to its "head." His violation of the covenant of nature *implicated* all his descendants.[36]

But the legal interpretation was, in turn, modified and rejected by a number of later writers. Among them, the Presbyterian Richard Baxter drew an analogy between the political idea of the social contract and the theory of imputation. In so doing, he introduced the notion of "personal consent" to the discussion; we are members of society by consent, and this means that we must "bear or venture on the common inconveniences and infelicity of that Society." And as a logical consequence of this it is "by their own consent fundamentally, that such persons, though innocent themselves are made liable to punishment."[37] It appears, therefore, that the notion of an *animal unum*, which we saw in the ancient Greek conception of ancestral fault and which reappeared in many Christian interpretations of original sin, was challenged by what one might call a civic notion of corporate responsibility.

34 Ibid., 202.

35 Ibid., 198. This was not a purely English discussion. He also notes the influence of writers outside of England, especially Arminius and Josué de la Place, on these discussions.

36 Ibid., 200–1.

37 Baxter cited in Heyd, "Original Sin, the Struggle for Stability," 205.

These terms reflected the emerging liberal political sensibilities of the time. The most influential person "in the long term" to write on this topic in the late seventeenth century was, of course, John Locke, who, according to Heyd, went further than Baxter and rejected the imputation account of original sin and the analogy with the social contract. Although Heyd does not remark upon this fact, it is interesting to note that Locke made use of a temporal argument to do so: "Some men would have all Adam's Posterity doomed to Eternal Infinite Punishment for the Transgression of Adam, whom Millions had never heard of, and no one had authorized to transact for him, or be his Representative."[38] If one holds the view that humans descending from Adam are a single organism, then it might make sense to view the transmission of his original sin as matter of inheritance. But if Adam is viewed as a representative of man, then the matter becomes more complex; after all, how can authorization be transmitted retroactively across thousands of years? Temporal distance becomes a more significant factor in the latter case. Heyd cites the following statement from Locke's follower, Thomas Chubb, without noting that the logic of his argument is also informed by a belief in the importance of temporal distance: "How Unequal must it be for us to be chargeable with that Guilt which was contracted five Thousand Years before we were born."[39] If guilt is understood as being "contracted" and "charged" to later generations, it raises the question of how long obligations can reasonably be said to persist. The suggestion that they might extend over thousands of years also appeared offensive to another reader of John Locke, the eighteenth-century British wine merchant Pentecost Barker. The historian Matthew Kadane seeks to illustrate how liberal and Enlightenment ideas were picked up and adopted by the broader population by presenting a case study of this little-known man born in Plymouth in 1690. Barker underwent a personal transformation during his life, gradually rejecting elements of the Reformed tradition and embracing Enlightenment thought. One of his concerns was the doctrine of original sin, in one of his letters to a heterodox minister called Samuel Merivale, Barker wrote: "And what's the English of this, but that I was then in the Loins of Adam, & sinned, as he did, tho I knew nothing of it

38 Locke, *The Reasonableness of Christianity*, cited ibid., 207.
39 Chubb, cited ibid., 209.

till 5000 years after? Is it any wonder that a Man of sense turns Deist?"[40] From the other side of the debate, and outside of the English context, Blaise Pascal defended the doctrine of original sin against temporal arguments like these in his *Pensées*. That text, which was composed in the midst of a controversy between Jesuits and Jansenists and published posthumously in 1670, included a response to what must have been a very common objection to the doctrine:

> Without doubt nothing is more shocking to our reason than to say that the sin of the first man has implicated in its suit men so far from the original sin that they seem incapable of sharing it. This flow of guilt does not seem merely impossible to us, but indeed most unjust. What could be more contrary to the rules of our miserable justice than the eternal damnation of a child, incapable of will, for an act in which he seems to have had so little part that it was actually committed 6,000 years before he existed? Certainly nothing jolts us more rudely than this doctrine, and yet but for this mystery, the most incomprehensible of all, we remain incomprehensible to ourselves.[41]

The disputes about original sin took place against the background of a complex web of cultural changes during the same period, in which the nature of the self and its relation to society were important topics of discussion. Heyd, for his part, argues that the transformation of the doctrine reflects a broader intellectual turn characterized by a new sense of individualism in Britain. This new "moral individualism," Heyd warns us, must not be confused with the thesis of "possessive individualism" advanced most famously by C. B. Macpherson.[42] But he does not elaborate upon how exactly the moral individualism he describes differs from the view that, with the rise of market society in the seventeenth century, liberal philosophers like Hobbes and Locke began to describe the individual as a proprietor of his (they spoke only of men) own person and present human relations as transactional. In fact, Heyd's account seems

40 Pentecost Barker to Samuel Merivale, May 24, 1762, cited in Kadane, "Original Sin and the Path to the Enlightenment," 105.

41 Pascal, cited in Jacobs, *Original Sin*, 117–18.

42 Heyd, "Original Sin, the Struggle for Stability," 220–1; C. B. Macpherson, *The Political Theory of Possessive Individualism: Hobbes to Locke* (Oxford: Oxford University Press, 1962).

perfectly congruent with Macpherson's argument that, in the period under discussion (in England at least), human relations were being construed in the language of an economic system of private property and market exchange.

The recurrent invocation of temporal distance across these admittedly very different examples, also merits further reflection. It is tempting to read them as yet more evidence in support of Koselleck's narrative, according to which conceptions of time and history underwent important transformations during the same period. Reinhart Koselleck and, following him, François Hartog and Zachary S. Schiffman, among others, have emphasized that this drawn-out process involved the erosion of prevailing Christian notions of history.[43] Two events, the Reformation and the Peace of Augsburg, made it possible for a conceptual split to begin to emerge between a secular time of politics and the previously encompassing view of history as salvation—a development crystalized in the work of Jean Bodin, who was able to speak about "sacral, human and natural history."[44] The nature of sacred time continued to be subject to debate and revision as the end of the world appeared to have been "prorogued."[45] This postponement also coincided with the emergence of new predictions, rooted in astrological observation, about the apocalypse, which expanded the time frame considerably.[46]

What is neglected by these historians of temporality is that the development of a novel understanding of historical time was also generated, in no small part, by the coming to dominance of a new mode of production and distribution. What Karl Polanyi called the market society did not simply produce a different sense of individualism—whether possessive or moral—it also permitted what Jacques Le Goff calls "merchant time" to take precedence over "church time."[47] Tony Claydon explains that this process reached something of a culmination point in England

43 François Hartog, *Regimes of Historicity: Presentism and Experiences of Time*, trans. S. Brown (New York: Columbia University Press, 2015), 201; Zachary Sayre Schiffman, *The Birth of the Past* (Baltimore, MD: Johns Hopkins University Press, 2011).

44 Ibid.

45 Reinhart Koselleck, *Futures Past*, trans. Keith Tribe (New York: Columbia University Press, 2004), 15.

46 Koselleck notes—incorrectly—that Isaac Newton predicted that the world would end in 2000, ibid.

47 Jacques Le Goff, *Time, Work, and Culture in the Middle Ages* (Chicago: University of Chicago Press, 1980), 29.

toward the end of the seventeenth century, when the social, economic, political, and cultural changes of the foregoing years worked to "empty chronology of divinity" so that "days and years were now structured, not by the rituals of the church, but rather by the demands of the state and an emerging capitalist economy. Such duties as arriving at work on time or paying taxes or rents on a set date replaced spiritual festivals as temporal markers."[48]

John Pocock ventures an even bolder claim when he writes that "the sense of a secular future is the child of capitalist investment."[49] The national debt and the expansion of credit that went with this required individuals not only to think of one another as trustworthy people to lend to but also to have an expectation that there was a capacity to grow and develop economic activity, to make good on their financial speculations, thus leading to an entirely new "ideology" of a "secular and historical future."[50]

> Without belief in the progress of the arts, the investing mercantile society literally could not maintain itself. But in what was belief in such a future to be rooted? Not in experience, since there is no way of experiencing a future; not in reason . . . not in Christian faith, since the most apocalyptic of prophecies is not concerned to reveal the future state of the market.[51]

Borrowing Koselleck's vocabulary, we might say that Pocock explains how the expansion of capitalist credit led to a break between the space of experience and horizon of expectation. Speculation involves the opening up of the future to the fantasy and imagination of the creditor (though for the debtor, the horizon of expectation is fixed and determined as one of scheduled repayment). But did this financial sensibility also have an effect on the perception of the past?[52] The answer, I think,

48 Tony Claydon, *The Revolution in Time: Chronology, Modernity, and 1688–1689 in England* (Oxford: Oxford University Press, 2020), 7.

49 John Pocock, *Virtue, Commerce, and History: Essays on Political Thought and History, Chiefly in the Eighteenth Century* (Cambridge: Cambridge University Press, 1985), 69.

50 Ibid., 98.

51 Ibid.

52 During the same period, Newtonian time—linear and homogeneous—entered the picture: a mathematical and indifferent view of time that differed significantly from the religious notions and ideas about time.

is yes. Because, during the same period and after, as I will explain below, intergenerational bonds were rearticulated in the language of property, of capitalist money, and of national belonging.

Debt and money

It has often been noted that the concepts of sin, guilt, and debt are intertwined. The sociologist Geoffrey Ingham explains: "In all Indo-European languages, words for 'debt' are synonymous with those for 'sin' or 'guilt,' illustrating the links between religion, payment and the mediation of the sacred and profane realms by 'money.'"[53] The financial and moral connotations of the term "debt" are also clearly in evidence in the discourse around reparations for slavery. The bold title of Randall Robinson's best-selling book *The Debt: What America Owes to Blacks* announces a case that is at once moral and financial.[54]

Reparations activists are likely well aware of the very long history of the intergenerational transmission of debts. It is a tradition that goes back to the beginning of recorded history in ancient Mesopotamia. One could say that there is a certain ironic reversal implicit in reparations claims which use the rhetoric of debt, because, throughout history, debt has served as one of the primary mechanisms for coercing people into slavery. This enslavement could be passed down from generation to generation. Indeed, some have argued that debt was invented in the ancient Near East as a means of obtaining labor power.[55] Debt was heritable in other regions as well; the concept was recognized in Roman law and in the biblical tradition.[56] Recall that Gagné argued that ancient Greeks did not always seem to draw a clear distinction between moral and financial heredity. But, at the same time, there was also an important tradition of debt forgiveness—taken

53 Geoffrey Ingham, *The Nature of Money* (Cambridge: Polity, 2004), 272, ebook.

54 Randall Robinson, *The Debt: What America Owes to Blacks* (New York: Dutton, 2000).

55 P. Steinkeller makes this argument, elaborating on a claim made by M. Finley, in M. Hudson and M. Van De Mieroop, eds., *Debt and Economic Renewal in the Ancient Near East* (Bethesda, MD: CDL Press, 2002), 111.

56 A. Riggsby, "Inheritance," in *Roman Law and the Legal World of the Romans* (Cambridge: Cambridge University Press, 2010), 153–64.

over from earlier ancient Middle Eastern civilizations—the well-known idea of the jubilee. So, once again, we see that the question of heredity presented a dilemma. Two competing ideas about debt and its transmission existed side by side: one in which debts should be paid, and the other in which they should be forgiven. As David Graeber has argued, however, even though both principles have long lineages and were often invoked, power relations have tended to determine which one is actually practiced.[57]

The ideas about debt and inheritance were well known to the Early Modern thinkers discussed above. And yet at the very same moment that the notion that *moral* responsibility—whether in the form of guilt, sin, or punishment—could be transmitted across generations was rejected, *monetary* and *contractual* links across generations were explicitly defended. Two of the main liberal thinkers to argue against inherited guilt—Hugo Grotius and John Locke—also defended the transmission of wealth and debt from one generation to the next.

Gagné argues that the Arminian convictions of Hugo Grotius—and, thus, his view on original sin—shaped his understanding of the Greek idea of ancestral fault, and informed his rejection of the idea that guilt could be inherited. Grotius's master work, *De iure belli ac pacis*, drew on the classical tradition and was deeply influenced by his reading of Plutarch's *De sera numinis vindicta* regarding the issue of punishment.[58] Grotius could not easily dismiss the ideas of inherited guilt and punishment, since he was aware that they had a long and venerable history. Simply invoking temporal distance to ridicule the notion would not suffice. Instead, he made a careful argument in which he relied on a series of careful and important distinctions. Key among these was the distinction between human and divine law. Discerning these two spheres allowed him to reject the notion of punishment across generations in human terms while simultaneously recognizing that God might still choose to punish across generations if and when he sees fit. But in making this seemingly simple argument, the Dutch scholar engaged in some impressive logical acrobatics. In chapter 21 of *De iure*, Grotius considered the question of collective responsibility using the example of a corporation—a matter of no small importance for the man who had

57 David Graeber, *Debt: The First 5000 Years* (Brooklyn: Melville House, 2011).

58 Gagné, *Ancestral Fault*, 98.

been a political advisor to the Vereenigde Oost-Indische Compagnie (Dutch East India Company or VOC). He admits that corporations can persist over time and can thus be held responsible for actions over an extended period. However, Grotius claimed that a corporation is composed of individuals, and it is these individuals who remain *imputable* for their own actions. Personal responsibility is essential for punishment, and thus, he argued, when all the individual members of a corporate group die, it is no longer permissible to punish that corporation. Here, Grotius explicitly rejected Plutarch's view on this same issue saying that it contradicts natural law.[59]

So far so good: Grotius's rejection of inherited punishment on the grounds of individual responsibility seems clear, consistent, and not dissimilar to the English arguments we reviewed earlier. But, as Gagné shows, Grotius was obliged to deal with some obvious exceptions to his, *prima facie*, simple argument. First, he had to deal with the issue of inherited merits. Here he directly tackled the contradiction Sarkozy would avoid dealing with centuries later. If it is unjust for punishment to be handed down from father to son, then it might also seem logical that merits cannot be passed down either. Not so, according to Grotius, for the simple reason that "benefits are of such a nature, by their matter, that they may be bestowed upon anyone without injury, but punishments are not."[60] Gagné reads this line as a defense of noble privilege and heredity honor.

Some contemporary readers might find Grotius's statement that inherited benefits do not harm others less dubious than I do. But, I imagine, most readers would likely perceive a pure contradiction in the Dutch scholar's emphatic rejection of inherited punishment while simultaneously supporting the inheritance of slaves. To Grotius, slavery is not a form of punishment but a form of "dominion."[61] Masters have dominion over their slaves just as fathers over their children and wives. Dominion can be passed down while punishment cannot. The distinction between punishment and dominion enabled Grotius to make a third point as well. Gagné notes how "the Arminian," who rejected the prevailing notions of original sin in his day, dealt with passages in the

59 Ibid., 102.
60 Cited in Gagné, *Ancestral Fault*, 103.
61 Ibid., 104.

Bible—discussed above—that appear to support the idea that God can punish children for the sins of the fathers. He can do so not because any "pollution or taint" is handed down, but because:[62]

> God has the most plenary right of dominion, as over our goods, so over our lives, as a gift: which he may take away from any one, whenever he will, and without any cause. If therefore, he takes away, by an untimely and violent death, the children of Achan, Saul, Jeroboam, Achab, he uses toward them his right of dominion, not of punishment.[63]

Because God has dominion over us, he can do whatever he pleases with us and our descendants. Likewise, in the realm of mortals, dominion (over enslaved people, among others) can also be handed down (presumably as a "benefit" that "harms no one") whereas punishment cannot. It appears that the right of ownership is such that it can transform a violent act from a punishment into the withdrawal of a gift. It is difficult not to read this position as a legal defense of the social and economic "interests of the Dutch commercial empire and its urban patriciate"; a task to which Ellen M. Wood claims Grotius devoted his entire life.[64]

A final step in Grotius's argument involves another distinction, this time between debt and demerit. Gagné's review of Grotius's rejection of ancestral fault does not discuss a key part of the section which provides most of the material and classical references for his analysis; paragraph 19 of chapter 21 of book 2 of *De iure belli ac pacis* deals with the question of inherited debts. For Grotius, it was clear and well established that debts can be inherited:

> The Heir does not represent the Deceased in his Deserts or Demerits, which are Qualities merely personal, but only his Effects; and in these, upon this Principle that at one and the same Time that Property was

62 Ibid., 110.

63 Grotius, *De Iure*, book 2, chapter 21.14 cited ibid., 106.

64 Ellen M. Wood, *Liberty and Property: A Social History of Western Political Thought from the Renaissance to Enlightenment* (London: Verso, 2012), 119. Also on page 121, "Grotius's major works elaborated an ideology well suited to 'extra economic' strategies for establishing commercial supremacy; and they were transparently constructed to defend the very particular practices of the Dutch in their quest for commercial domination, not least by means of war."

> introduced, it was made an established Law that the Debts which arise from the Inequality of Things should be attached to them. Thus Dion Prusaensis (Dion of Prusa, or Dio Chrysostomus) in his Rhodiaca ἅπαντα ὀφείλουσι, &c. *What was due from Predecessors is no less due from their Posterity. For you cannot say that we have renounced our Succession.*[65]

The distinction Grotius draws here, which goes against the tendency, described above by Ingham, to conflate debt with sin and guilt, enabled him to reject the inheritance of guilt but defend the inheritance of property and debt.

John Locke, whose criticism of the notion of inherited sin we have already discussed, made a similar distinction. While rejecting original sin, he simultaneously formulated a theory of intergenerational obligation in the language of money. Joshua Foa Dienstag noted the central role money plays in the Locke's *Second Treatise*, which contested existing histories of political authority.[66] His famous argument about the state of nature was a response to Robert Filmer, who, in *Patrarchia*, presented political authority as descending from Adam.[67] Locke offered an alternative "plot" which begins with God's creation of humanity and reaches a turning point—Dienstag calls it an "overture"—when money comes on to the scene. Prior to the introduction of money, human interactions did not take a contractual form. But money changed this:

> Only money allows for the fulfillment of agreements to be deferred over any length of time. Each coin is a mini pledge and the fabric of society is maintained only through the integrity of such pledges. Without money, an integrated society would not be possible, and government, which follows upon that society, would not be necessary.[68]

65 Hugo Grotius, *The Rights of War and Peace*, book 2, ed. Richard Tuck (Indianapolis: Liberty Fund, 2005), 1094–5, italics in original.

66 Joshua F. Dienstag, "Between History and Nature: Social Contract Theory in Locke and the Founders," *Journal of Politics* 58, no. 4 (1996), 987.

67 Ibid., 987.

68 Ibid., 988.

Accordingly, men came together to form the social contract voluntarily; but this raised the question of how each generation could be bound to said contract if they did not consent to it. How can the contractual form of the government persist across time? "The key, unsurprisingly, is property." Locke recast the social contact as a "testament" to construct a link between the founders of a society and later generations.[69] Men hold property under the laws of the political community. When future descendants are born, they cannot be forced to join the social contract, but if individuals accept inheritance, they are also obliged to abide by the conditions that come with it. Thus conceived, the social contract becomes like a "large will for all inheritors in its domain."[70] While guilt cannot have been handed down from the time of Adam, property, through the bonds of money and contract, can be handed down over the centuries. In the logic of the emerging capitalist system, it is money that unites society across and within time.

The fact that liberal philosophers articulated intergenerational relations in financial terms may explain why contemporary political philosophers writing in the same tradition have a difficult time expounding a theory of moral responsibility for historical injustice but have a comparatively easier time making financial arguments for reparations. Bernard Boxill is one philosopher who has shown that it is possible to make a relatively simple "inheritance"-based argument in Lockean terms. It involves advocating a form of reparations in which contemporary descendants of slaves would be allowed to collect the compensation that should have been paid to their ancestors.[71] Reparations claims that target corporations with links to slavery or individuals on the grounds that the fortunes they inherited were amassed with slave labor are thus rooted in a well-established liberal view of inheritance.[72] In this sense, Walter

69 Ibid., 990.

70 Ibid.

71 Bernard Boxill, "A Lockean Argument for Black Reparations," *Journal of Ethics* 7, no. 1 (2003): 63–91. Also see, Daniel Butt, "Inheriting Rights to Reparation: Compensatory Justice and the Passage of Time," *Ethical Perspectives* 20, no. 2 (2013): 245–69. And Jonathan Stanhope, "Hierarchies of Connection: On the Inheritance Argument for Slavery Reparations," *Jurisprudence* 12, no. 2 (2021): 200–25.

72 "Esclavagisme: Le CRAN demande reparation au baron Ernest-Antoine Seillière," *Sud Ouest*, May 9, 2015, sudouest.fr.

Benn Michaels is right when he criticizes reparations for slavery as being fundamentally a "liberal" idea.[73]

To be sure, so-called inheritance-based arguments for slavery reparations have faced criticisms from other liberal philosophers on a number of grounds. Some have suggested that the task of reconstructing what specific individuals and corporations inherited wealth from slavery would be a difficult, if not impossible, task after so many generations. Historical research projects such as the Legacies of British Slavery at University College London, however, have shown that this may not be as impossible as some would have us believe. It may simply require the political will to investigate the wealthy and powerful, and to attempt to penetrate the maze of blind trusts and other mechanisms that they use to disguise the extent of their assets. Yet even if that could be achieved, coming to a just accounting of the inherited wealth and debt would still be no easy matter, as I will explain in more detail in the next chapter.

Janna Thompson's critiques of the "inheritance arguments" for reparations highlight serious moral problems. She rightly points out that the argument would produce a very narrow conception of reparations based on property, and this would mean that no damages could be claimed for the horrors of slavery that were not directly quantifiable in financial terms. But the excessive focus on money and property is perhaps not so much a weakness of inheritance-based claims for slavery reparations as it is a defect of liberal ideology in general.

National responsibility

David Miller criticizes Janna Thompson's argument, saying that

> her underlying aim is not justice but *reconciliation*—or to put it more exactly, the redress of past injustice as a means of achieving reconciliation. This is a worthwhile aim, certainly, but it bypasses the question whether we can inherit responsibilities that impose *obligations of justice* on the present generation.[74]

73 Jacobin, "The Uses (and Abuses) of History—Adolph Reed & Walter Benn Michaels," YouTube, August 6, 2021, youtube.com.

74 David Miller, *National Responsibility and Global Justice* (Oxford: Oxford University Press, 2012), 146.

He notes the presence, in both common and Roman law traditions, of a notion of inherited responsibility.[75] But Miller's main argument is that reparations for historical injustices can be defended precisely on the principle of *national* responsibility. If one accepts the idea that one can inherit benefits as a member of a national collective, then it should follow that they can also inherit responsibilities. This would indeed be a consistent position and an alternative to Sarkozy's opportunistic invocation of national identity.

Nationalist thinkers, well before Sarkozy, presented contradictory views on the nature of heredity. The notion of collective responsibility, or even collective guilt, is a key component of nationalist thought; arguably the most important political idea of the modern period.[76] In times of war, patriotic appeals to "do your duty" for the nation or to protect the national honor are commonly invoked, and the language of inherited responsibility is articulated in no uncertain terms. Meanwhile, collective responsibility is regularly practiced—if not always expressed—in the yearly and daily activities of tax payment, which is often in the service of intergenerational obligations such as the repayment of national debt or the funding of pension systems. For centuries, the metropolitan centers of finance have regularly reminded countries on the (semi)periphery of the globalizing economy that they need to repay debts—even those incurred by previous generations. Why should reparations activists in these countries not make use of the same rhetoric?

75 He makes an interesting argument about what this would mean for reparations: "Both common and Roman law, then, accept the core idea that those who inherit from wrongdoers are potentially liable to make compensation for the wrongs committed. What has to be shown is that the victims or their descendants are themselves made worse off by the effects of the wrong—it is the failure of this condition that presumably excludes defamation as a cause of action under common law. On the other hand, the law insists that inheritors not be *punished* for what their predecessors did, and so this sets an upper limit to the compensation that must be paid. The common law does this by interpreting the claim for compensation as a claim against A's estate: A's successors are not liable to contribute resources that they own independently of the inheritance. Roman law dispensed with this safeguard, but instead allowed the designated heir to decide whether to assume that office." Ibid., 150.

76 The periodization of the emergence of nationalism has been a point of contention among historians of the idea. The dominant view in contemporary historiography is that nationalism is a modern idea. While I do not deny that certain elements of modern nationalism existed long before modernity, I want to focus here on how nationalism was articulated in the modern period.

The very idea of the nation would be unthinkable without notions of collective bonds of duty and responsibility that are both synchronic and diachronic in kind. That is why Benedict Anderson's explication of the imagined community underscores the fact that temporal relations of simultaneity and continuity across generations are constitutive of this concept. "The idea of a sociological organism moving calendrically through homogeneous, empty time is a precise analog of the idea of the nation, which also is conceived as a solid community moving steadily down (or up) history."[77] In this conception, then, the idea of liberal individuality described above is superseded by a conception of an individual as an element of a collective—a transhistorical organism that is remarkably similar to the *animal unum* which Proclus described as "homochronous."

Whether articulated in cultural/ethnic or in civic terms, modern nationalisms tend to extol the virtues of individual responsibility, and even of sacrifice, for the collective. For Fichte, the permanence of the individual could be achieved through the continuity of the nation. A noble man knows that "permanence is promised to him only by the independent perpetuation of his nation; to save it he must be willing even to die, so that it may live."[78] Meanwhile, for Ernest Renan, too, the nation must be understood as a "spiritual principle" that is founded on a "rich legacy of memories" and "the desire to continue to invest in the heritage that we have jointly received." This involves love and sacrifice of each generation:

> A nation is therefore a vast solidarity, constituted by the sentiment of the sacrifices one has made and of those one is yet prepared to make. It presupposes a past; it is, however, summarized in the present by a tangible fact: consent, the clearly expressed desire to continue a common life. A nation's existence is (if you will pardon the metaphor) an everyday plebiscite, just as an individual's existence is a perpetual affirmation of life.[79]

77 Benedict Anderson, *Imagined Communities: Reflections on the Origin and Spread of Nationalism* (London: Verso, 2016), 26.

78 Gregory Moore, *Fichte: Addresses to the German Nation* (Cambridge: Cambridge University Press, 2009), 104.

79 Ernest Renan, "What Is a Nation? (Qu'est-ce qu'une nation?, 1882)," in *What Is a Nation? and Other Political Writings* (New York: Columbia University Press, 2018), 217.

Bonds of unity throughout time are thus the very essence of nationality and indeed a certain immortality is provided to us through national belonging. That is precisely the point and the benefit of participation and the reason why one is supposed to embrace what is inherited from previous generations. On the other hand, Renan was well aware of the risks involved in fully taking up the weight of the national past:

> The act of forgetting, I would even say, historical error, is an essential factor in the creation of a nation, which is why progress in historical studies often constitutes a danger for nationality. Indeed, historical enquiry brings back to light the deeds of violence that took place at the origin of all political formations, even of those whose consequences have been the most beneficial. Unity is always achieved brutally.[80]

It is no wonder that the right wing today sees history departments as such a menace.

Vaunting the national past or laying claim to national inheritance has always been a double-edged sword. This dilemma is hardly new, and nationalist thinkers have always had to come up with ways to lay claim to the glories of the past while rejecting responsibility for its evils. The great conservative and nationalist thinker Edmund Burke, whose ideas have influenced subsequent generations of conservatives down to the present, provides an interesting example. He is mostly remembered for his robust defense of the importance of tradition. One of the main points of Burke's writing on the French Revolution was to argue that it was incorrect to compare it to the English Revolution of 1688. The English example was superior, he said, because of its rootedness in respect for tradition rather than in abstract notions of reason:

> In the famous law of the 3rd of Charles I., called the Petition of Right, the parliament says to the king, "Your subjects have inherited this freedom," claiming their franchises not on abstract principles "as the rights of men," but as the rights of Englishmen, and as a patrimony derived from their forefathers.

80 Ibid., 209.

And, later

> You will observe, that from Magna Charta to the Declaration of Right it has been the uniform policy of our constitution to claim and assert our liberties, as an entailed inheritance derived to us from our forefathers, and to be transmitted to our posterity; as an estate specially belonging to the people of this kingdom, without any reference whatever to any other more general or prior right. By this means our constitution preserves a unity in so great a diversity of its parts. We have an inheritable crown; an inheritable peerage; and a House of Commons and a people inheriting privileges, franchises, and liberties, from a long line of ancestors.[81]

Liberty, for the English, is a matter of inheritance passed down since the Magna Carta. Here, his defense of intergenerational transmission could hardly be more emphatic. But what did Burke make of inherited responsibility?

Readers of John Torpey's widely read book on reparations politics may be surprised to find that the author starts his critique of reparations politics by holding up Edmund Burke as an example of an early and eloquent critic of "dredging up old wrongs for political purposes."[82] The long citation of Burke's *Reflections on the French Revolution* does read like a prescient objection to reparations for slavery:

> It is not very just to chastise men for the offenses of their natural ancestors; but to take the fiction of ancestry in a corporate succession, as a ground for punishing men who have no relation to guilty acts, except in names and general descriptions, is a sort of refinement of injustice belonging to the philosophy of this enlightened age . . . Corporate bodies are immortal for the good of the members, but not for their punishment. Nations themselves are such corporations.[83]

81 Ibid.

82 John Torpey, *Making Whole What Has Been Smashed: On Reparations Politics* (New Brunswick, NJ: Rutgers University Press, 2017), 10.

83 Burke cited in ibid., 10.

Why are corporate bodies immortal for good and not for punishment? Unlike Grotius, Torpey does not investigate this question any further. He appears to cite Burke simply to make the point that assertions of intergenerational guilt have always been ridiculed, but he does not seem to notice the apparent inconsistency in Burke's view on tradition which bears a remarkable similarity to Sarkozy's more recent statements about reparations and national identity.

The persistence of sin

If there was a widespread rejection of original sin during the Enlightenment, notions of inherited obligations in the form of capitalist money and property and national belonging persisted. But the idea of original sin did not entirely disappear from political discourse. Measuring the extent of popular rejection of the doctrine is beyond the scope of this study—if it is possible at all. What can be said, however, is that conservative and counter-Enlightenment thinkers like Edmund Burke and Joseph de Maistre continued to use the notion of original sin well into the nineteenth century. Burke contested the Enlightenment rejection of original sin, and the belief in the fallibility of humans was a key element of his political thinking. He held that "the inclinations of men should frequently be thwarted, their will controlled, and their passions brought into subjection."[84] Maistre's arguments also influenced numerous subsequent conservative thinkers, including Carl Schmitt, who discusses the idea of original sin in *Political Theology*.[85] The thrust of his argument is to suggest that anarchists and conservatives have different views of human nature.

---

84 Edmund Burke, *Reflections on the Revolution in France: In a Letter Intended to Have Been Sent to a Gentleman in Paris*, 1790, available at Pepperdine School of Public Policy, publicpolicy.pepperdine.edu.

85 Carl Schmitt, *Political Theology: Four Chapters on the Concept of Sovereignty*, trans. George Schwab (Chicago: University of Chicago Press, 2005 [1922]), 57. This comes in the context of Schmitt's discussion of the counterrevolutionary philosophy of the state (p. 56) in which he explains that "every political idea in one way or another takes a position on the 'nature' of man and presupposes that he is either 'by nature good' or 'by nature evil.'" He goes on to argue that reactionaries like Donoso Cortés were informed by a radical view of the doctrine of original sin and view human nature as depraved. Anarchists by contrast have a view of human nature as good.

It is quite likely that Karl Jaspers would have been well aware of Schmitt's invocation of original sin when he wrote about German guilt after the war. If so, then it would be tempting to view Jaspers's reflections on this topic as—at least in part—a response to this line of thinking. After all, the notion of metaphysical guilt clearly echoes the doctrine of original sin and the debates about human nature: "If human beings were able to free themselves from metaphysical guilt, they would be angels, and all the other three concepts of guilt would be immaterial."[86] When, at the start of his essay, Jaspers explains the four different kinds of guilt—criminal, political, moral, and metaphysical—he notes where jurisdiction rests in each case. In the final case, "jurisdiction rests with God alone."[87] It seems logical to try to interpret Jaspers's writing on guilt against the background of the historical context he confronted; the Nazi period, when the concepts of tradition and inheritance of the German nation were constantly invoked, and when preeminent philosophers such as Martin Heidegger held guilt/debt (*Schuld*) to be central to human existence.[88]

In a very different context, Touré Reed has noted how the phrase "original sin" is used to describe the relationship of the United States with slavery. But, Reed suggests, if one believes—as some Christians do—that only grace can save humanity from sin, then this may lead one to the politically paralyzing position that nothing can be done to ameliorate the legacy of slavery and racism in America.[89] When Obama called slavery America's "original sin" in his 2008 speech on race, he must have been aware how the large part of the American electorate that was deeply religious would perceive the reference. He himself claimed to be inspired by the political ideas of Christian realism, in which the belief in the sinfulness of humanity plays a central role. As Reinhold Niebuhr—the thinker with whom this political theological tradition is most often

86 Karl Jaspers, *The Question of German Guilt*, trans. E. B. Ashton (New York: Fordham University Press, 2000), 27.

87 Ibid., 26.

88 After the war, Heidegger would reject Jaspers's notion of metaphysical guilt. For an investigation of the relationship between Heidegger's notion of *Schuld* and the theological concept of sin, see Yu-Yuan Hung, "Heidegger's Understanding of the Relation Between His Ontological Concept of 'Being-Guilty' and Luther's Theological Concept of 'Sin,'" *International Journal of Philosophy and Theology* 81, no. 2 (2020): 120–35.

89 *The Michael Brooks Show*, "Why Touré Reed Never Wants to Hear the Phrases 'Structural Racism' and 'White Privilege,'" YouTube, December 28, 2020, youtube.com.

associated—once remarked, "The doctrine of original sin is the only empirically verifiable doctrine of the Christian faith."[90]

When reparations advocates speak of slavery as an original sin, of the existence of a debt that has been handed down from the past, they are drawing on ideas that have existed for millennia. Those calling for reparations for slavery do not, in general, seek to establish new political norms—a politics of the past or of regret—nor do they want to articulate a new ethics of intergenerational relations; rather, they seek only to use existing and well-established ideas in order to legitimate their very particular claims about slavery and colonialism. Usually, they do not express a view about how societies should deal with all historic injustices in general.

Those who are concerned that the payment of reparations for slavery would unfairly burden children with the task of making amends for the misdeeds of their ancestors should, at the very least, recognize that this question has been dealt with before, and that it goes well beyond the issue of reparations for slavery. As we have seen, the idea that current generations can be held responsible for past misdeeds has an ancient lineage going back to ancient Greece, if not before, and that continued into early modern Europe. While some early liberal political thinkers rejected the notion of inherited guilt, they allowed for the intergenerational transmission of obligations through property, money, testament, and trusts. They replaced older notions of inherited guilt and sin with conceptions of intergenerational bonds in the form of national belonging, money, and property. During the same period, however, the curse of Ham was still used to rationalize the enslavement of parents and children. The notion of intergenerational corporate responsibility was also reaffirmed by conservative and anti-Enlightenment thinkers and became a core component of modern nationalist thought. In short, political thought in the West has produced ambiguous, confused, and sometimes contradictory ideas about intergenerational relations. There is no clear and coherent Western idea about how intergenerational relations should be conceived. From this perspective, the debates about reparations for slavery can be seen, at least in part, as a recent manifestation of an age-old conundrum about the right way to conceive of intergenerational relations.

---

90 Niebuhr purported to have read this quip in the *Times Literary Supplement*. Cited in Derek Nelson, *Sin: A Guide for the Perplexed* (London: Bloomsbury, 2011), 36.

This is not to say that these views of intergenerational relations are necessarily and always morally sound. It is only to say that they are generally adhered to in the societies in which claims for reparations have been made. And that is precisely the point that, I believe, reparations advocates make. They know that such claims are unpopular in societies that have benefited from slavery and colonialism, and that might stand to lose a great deal from acknowledging that fact. Using existing mechanisms and principles to obtain some amount of material compensation is therefore primarily a strategic choice. Some may argue that this is the wrong strategy. But what these critics should note is that it is indeed *a* strategy and one that is intended to succeed in a world in which liberal and nationalist ideas are recognized by dominant states and institutions of power, and in which the ideas of the classical world, along with those passed down in the traditions of the Abrahamic religions, continue to resonate with large numbers of people.

4

Value in Time and Time as Value

The profits of a sugar-plantation in any of our West Indian colonies are generally much greater than those of any other cultivation that is known either in Europe or America.
—Adam Smith, *The Wealth of Nations*

In 1800 the average income per person per day all over the planet . . . was in present-day money, anything from $1 to $5. Call it an average of $3 a day . . . That's three-fourths of a cappuccino at Starbucks. It was and is appalling.
—Deirdre McCloskey, *Why Liberalism Works*

In interest bearing capital . . . this automatic fetish is elaborated into its pure form, self-valorizing value, money breeding money, and in this form it no longer bears any marks of its origin. The social relation is consummated in the relationship of a thing, money, to itself.
—Karl Marx, *Capital*, vol. 3

The time value of money

Opponents of reparations for slavery have sometimes argued that trying to ascribe monetary value to ineffable suffering is both vulgar and impossible. Aimé Césaire was reasoning along these lines when he said:

"Reparations for something that is irreparable and unquantifiable are impossible."[1] The eminent French legal scholar Antoine Garapon has suggested that the proliferation of movements advocating reparations for historical injustices indicates the increasing globalization, not only of American legal frameworks but also of American culture in which money is conflated with moral virtue. In America, "money is a sign of recognition and of moral election."[2]

But the proper target of this variety of criticism is not reparations claims per se (nor is it American culture). Rather, it is the conception of money and value that such claims would appear to require. The conception of money in which anything can be priced and thereby rendered commensurable with all other things on the market is called general-purpose money by economic anthropologists, following Karl Polanyi.[3] They argue that this way of understanding money is dominant in contemporary capitalist societies. In other societies, exchange was—and often still is—based on other practices, such as gift giving, or money was reserved for special purposes only, such as trading with other groups. In societies where general-purpose money is used, however, anything can be priced in money terms. Therefore, putting a price on past suffering may be crass but it is indeed *possible*; what makes it possible is the conception of money as a universal equivalent. This is not to say that attempts to price past suffering are desirable or can even succeed in reflecting or representing the evils of slavery in some accurate or morally acceptable way. It is only to say that a price to be paid for slavery could conceivably be calculated in societies that use general-purpose money, such as our own.

There has always been something abhorrent about general-purpose money. The idea that anything can be evaluated in money terms offends what many feel are elementary notions of decency. We regularly seek to shield certain domains of life from this logic. That some

1 Aimé Césaire, "Je ne suis pas pour la repentance ou les réparations," *L'express*, September 13, 2001, lexpress.fr (my translation).

2 Antoine Garapon, *Peut-on réparer l'Histoire? Colonisation, esclavage, Shoah* (Paris: Odile Jacob, 2008), 29 (my translation).

3 Karl Polanyi discusses all-purpose money and special-purpose money in "The Economy as Instituted Process," in Karl Polanyi, Conrad M. Arensberg, and Harry W. Pearson, eds., *Trade and Market in the Early Empires: Economies in History and Theory* (New York: Free Press, Collier-Macmillan, 1957), 243–70.

people are repulsed by the idea of putting a price on the horrors of slavery is one example of this, but there are many others. Laws and taboos against prostitution or the use of money to purchase merits and positions of honor are widespread in many societies. While, at the personal level, monetary interactions between family and friends are often frowned upon. When money enters the academy, safeguards against conflicts of interest are considered central to maintaining the integrity of scientific research. Some have argued that the penetration of the market dynamic into research poses a clear threat to scholarly production and scholarly virtues.[4] But what is so interesting about these examples is that the interdictions and taboos against using money in these domains are constantly threatened by the coercive force and temptation of money power. Even where most might agree that money should be kept out, it still seeps in. One reason that general-purpose money exerts this pressure is that its capacity as a universal equivalent is widely recognized even when an exchange is not carried out. In other words, we can easily consider what something should or would cost even if we are not prepared to actually pay for it. Moreover, people sometimes reflect upon the cost of *not* paying for something or of not undertaking some action. This is what economists might call opportunity costs.

The history of capitalism has been one of the relentless "subsumption" of nonmonetary domains of activity into the market dynamic: the incorporation of ever larger parts of the world into the capitalist world system through trade and imperial expansion, the enclosure of common spaces, or, more recently, the penetration of money into the domestic sphere—as care for elders and children has been privatized and cooking and cleaning outsourced to (precarious, low-paid, and racialized) workers—are but a few examples of this trend.[5] Throughout the history of the expansion of capital, people have lamented the increasing penetration of money into all areas of life and fulminated against its power to undermine, corrupt, and transgress moral and cultural norms. If money has this power, it is because it works as a universal equivalent; it

4 See Chris Lorenz, "If You're So Smart, Why Are You Under Surveillance?: Universities, Neoliberalism, and New Public Management," *Critical Inquiry* 38, no. 3 (2012): 599–629.

5 It is true that in many cases payment for such services replaced slave labor and other forms of servitude in which labor is coerced by nonmarket means.

facilitates a comparison of anything with anything else and all things with money.

Time itself is not exempt from this logic. The cardinal "sin" for historians is anachronism, as Marc Bloch famously wrote.[6] But comparing values across time is virtue itself to the financier. The same characteristics that permit general-purpose money to render commensurate all goods on the market can also be extended diachronically. Money appears to be able to reach across times and to compare different epochs as though they were all elements of the same regime of value. Under capitalism, general-purpose money plays a crucial role as a *temporal instrument*. If modern time can be thought of as empty and homogenous, it is because money has rendered it fungible.

"Time is money." This well-known expression may appear simplistic but is in fact a deeply insightful statement about the nature of money in modern capitalist societies. To be sure, there is something reductive in it, as the relationship between time and money is multifaceted and complex. Nevertheless, the links between money and time are so apparent in the contemporary world that many who hear this expression intuitively grasp its connotative content. We live in a world in which money is ubiquitous, if unevenly distributed, and the language of money is even more widespread: Money is ever present in daily discussions, in contemporary music and in art. It permeates our language in the form of metaphors and analogies, and according to the Supreme Court of the United States, it is speech.[7]

If "money makes the world go round" then any discussion of the politics of time should surely take money into account. Remarkably, however, money has never been given due attention in philosophical and historical studies of time and temporality. Reinhart Koselleck and François Hartog barely discuss money in their accounts of shifting experiences of time in modernity. Peter Osborne's book on the politics of time does mention money but hardly gives it a central place in his discussion. Paul Ricoeur, for his part, did not discuss money in

6 Marc Bloch, *Apologie pour l'histoire ou métier d'historien*, 2nd ed. (Paris: Librairie Armand Colin, 1952), available at Université du Quebec à Montreal, classiques .uqam.ca.

7 Because the Supreme Court referred to the First Amendment of the Constitution in deciding the case *Citizens United v. FEC* many commentators have described this decision as equating money with speech.

Time and Narrative, even though it could easily be included alongside the other "reflective instruments" which he suggests facilitate human reckoning with time. Moreover, many of the other reflective instruments that Ricoeur discusses—the clock and the calendar, for example—were disseminated and imposed by states and firms seeking to facilitate market distribution and capitalist investment and accumulation. Time consciousness was inculcated in so many communities through the disciplinary force of the factory production of commodities and the demands of global trade. These societal changes transformed the very experience of time for billions of humans. E. P. Thompson eloquently described the way in which this shift was perceived in England when he noted that "time is now currency: it is not passed but spent."[8]

Perhaps prior analyses of temporality have omitted money from the discussion because the question of what money is, and how it functions, has already been addressed in other fields. There is serious disagreement among scholars of all varieties—political economists, historians, anthropologists, sociologists—about the nature of money and its functions. These disagreements, in turn, touch upon a number of contentious issues, including inflation, monetary and fiscal policy, and matters pertaining to debt. The definition of money has implications for historical accounts of the emergence of markets, the question of how capitalism really operates and how we identify where economic power lies. Above all, the definition of money is linked to the problem of the nature of economic value itself. In short, a great deal is at stake in the contest to define money and explain its function.

In the literature on money and its uses in the contemporary world, the debate between those who adhere to what has sometimes been called a commodity view of money on the one hand (metallism) and those who argue for a view of money as credit (chartalism) on the other has been among the most contentious. These disputes touch upon the relationship between money and credit/debt, the role of the state in its creation, the function of barter and more. As Geoffrey Ingham has noted, each of these positions leads to a different and

8 E. P. Thompson, "Time, Work, Discipline, and Industrial Capitalism," *Past and Present* 38 (1967): 61.

"irreconcilable" understanding of money's key functions.[9] Those functions were listed by the American economist Francis Amasa Walker in 1878 as being four: Money is (1) a measure of account and value, (2) a means of payment, (3) a medium of exchange, and (4) a store of value. As Ingham notes, "This list is still found almost without exception in today's textbooks. Its longevity gives the impression that the money question has been settled, but this is far from the case."[10]

It is not my intention to summarize the debates about the functioning of money in this chapter. Rather, I want to explain that money has another function, one that is rarely discussed in that literature. I will argue that money also serves as an instrument of temporality that plays a central role in organizing, coordinating, and distributing time in modern capitalist economies. This is true regardless of whether one holds a commodity or a credit view of money, even if the temporal dimension is much clearer in the latter theory. If money is credit, then it is a promise to pay at a later date, and this promise is made across a given expanse of time. Theories about the cyclical nature of credit expansion and contraction of the type described by Hyman Minsky, are attuned to the diachronic fluctuations of money in a way that models which present money as a *numéraire* do not.

There are a number of obvious ways in which money and time are linked. The question of value across time is, for instance, central to any understanding of debt. Whether or not money is a form of debt, all agree that debt is ubiquitous and essential to the functioning of modern capitalism. Currently, household debt in the leading capitalist country, the United States, is valued at $17.94 trillion and national governments all over the world struggle under increasingly high debt burdens.[11] Today, more people face a horizon of expectation that is determined by the repayment of debts than ever before. In this period, which is sometimes referred to as an era of the financialization of capitalism, the potential change and fluctuations of the value in financial assets and liabilities

9 Geoffrey Ingham, *Money: Ideology, History, Politics* (Cambridge: Polity, 2020), 45, ebook.

10 Ibid., 33–4.

11 Federal Reserve Bank of New York, "Household Debt Rose Modestly; Delinquency Rates Remain Elevated," press release, November 13, 2024, newyorkfed.org.

across time are ceaselessly being computed by individuals and algorithms around the globe. High-speed trading accords important advantages which can make or break fortunes.

The link between time and money is manifest in a core principle in investing called the time value of money: The price of money now is compared to the price of money later. Present and future value calculations are regularly used to assess the cost of committing money to one or another project. These calculations, in turn, involve an estimation of the rate of interest. Economic actors under capitalism are constantly reflecting on and anticipating movements in rates of interest and making investment decisions based on their estimation of how things will change over time. Long-term rates of interest tend to be higher than short-term rates. There is disagreement in economic literature about how interest rates are determined in modern capitalist economies, but generally, it is thought of as being influenced by supply and demand of money. But since central banks have taken on a key role in manipulating interest and exchange rates, they are not fully determined by market mechanisms. Even so, monetary policy is also based on analyses that have retrospective and prognostic dimensions.

Committing money capital to projects—or saving it instead—always involves an anticipation of future conditions in the markets. Where capitalist modes of production are dominant, the future is always being calculated and compared to the present in money terms, and the horizon of expectation can be measured numerically in general-purpose money. In the previous chapter, I discussed John Pocock's claim that the financial revolution of the late seventeenth century contributed to the development of an idea of a secular historical future, because investment and speculation required a belief that economic growth necessary to render investments profitable would occur. Traditional views of temporality informed by a religious understanding of history and eschatological predictions of the end of times were of limited use for such ends. It was necessary to envision a future in financial terms. Comparing estimations of the future state of the market to present-day realities in this way may indeed have produced a picture of historical development. And this may very well may have encouraged practical belief in the idea of historical progress which became so central to European thought from the Enlightenment onward. But Pocock might have looked more closely at the role that a conception of money as a universal equivalent played in these developments. The dynamic he describes is facilitated by the fact that money's capacity to render things commensurate could be extended diachronically. He is, no doubt, correct that investors needed to expect a growth in future economic activity that would meet their investments. But, at some level, they would have thought of this growth in terms of money. An investment today should be worth more money in the future.

It is a simple matter to redirect this same logic toward the past and to think of economic value in previous epochs in relation to the present day. While some historians may find it uncomfortable to compare the world of Atlantic slavery and the trade in human beings to the vastly more complex and globalized era in which we now live, techniques of economic accounting can compare the past to the present precisely in monetary terms. Although this may be difficult to achieve, there are abundant examples in academic historiography and popular discourse on how to do just that. Historians can, and regularly do, convert prices of past historical periods into current-day dollars. One example of this, which I will discuss in more detail below, is the ongoing debate among historians about the correct way to calculate the profitability of Atlantic slavery and its impact on the economies of a number of countries.

It is sometimes stated that the idea of history as a singular, homogeneous, and progressive development has been abandoned in the wake of postmodernist critiques. But such statements overlook the persistence of the belief in progress in discourses of development, which remain influential and important in economic discussions. In popular culture, advocates of capitalism point to statistics about economic growth in order to support a rose-colored view of the world. These calculate development in terms of money, which serves as the marker and measure of progress: Global GDP seems to rise inexorably, and while stock markets appear more volatile, the general upward trend is clear over the long term; economic growth is undeniable even if the reasons for it are disputed.[12]

12 Gross domestic product (GDP) is a well-known concept in contemporary economics. It is the measure of the *monetary* value of goods and services produced in a particular economy.

But a recent article published in the journal *World Development* (2023) reviews and challenges the commonly articulated claim that the rise of capitalism after 1800 has led to a dramatic decline in extreme poverty. The authors, Dylan Sullivan and Jason Hickel, note that this argument, made famous by public intellectuals like Steven Pinker, Hans Rosling, and others who use such data to celebrate the status quo, relies on a graph composed by Martin Ravallion in 2016, drawing on other sources.[13] The graph "gives the impression that 90% of humanity was in 'extreme poverty' prior to the 1800s; i.e., living on less than the equivalent of $1.90 per day (using 2011 purchasing power parity [PPP]), a threshold associated with extreme calorie and nutrient deficits and an inability to access basic goods."[14] Sullivan and Hickel criticize the method involved in compiling such measures. In particular, they note how using GDP data fails to account for "non-commodity forms of provisioning" which, in noncapitalist societies, would, of course, have been widespread. They cite Ravallion's own acknowledgment of the problems involved in using national account statistics for historical arguments. He writes: "As an economy develops, the household-based production activities that are not measured in NAS become 'formalized,' imparting an upward bias to measured NAS growth rates for output."[15] In other words, the subsumption of more productive activity into the market economy appears as growth when, in fact, it could simply be that previously prevalent ways of producing and distributing goods and services—without the use of money—have been commodified and are thus counted for the first time. In this sense, the expansion of commodification and use of money appears synonymous with "development." As the authors of the article go on to argue, if one takes into account nonmarket activity, it is highly unlikely that extreme poverty was as widespread in precapitalist societies as Pinker, Rosling, and others claim. Moreover,

13 Dylan Sullivan and Jason Hickel, "Capitalism and Extreme Poverty: A Global Analysis of Real Wages, Human Height, and Mortality Since the Long 16th Century," *World Development* 161 (2023): 2. The authors assert that Ravallion draws on F. Bourguignon and C. Morrison, "Inequality Among World Citizens: 1820–1992," *American Economic Review* 92, no. 4 (2002): 727–44. Bourguignon and Morrison, in turn, relied upon GDP data drawn from A. Maddison, *Monitoring the World Economy* (Paris: OECD, 1995).

14 Sullivan and Hickel, "Capitalism and Extreme Poverty," 1.

15 Ravallion cited ibid., 2.

Sullivan and Hickel show that the expansion of capitalism into numerous areas of the world in the nineteenth century and beyond was associated with increasing *poverty* not enrichment. This picture changed, they argue, somewhat provocatively, only when socialistic policies were implemented.[16]

Sullivan and Hickel's article will doubtless attract criticism from other economic historians. It is beyond the scope of the present study to weigh the accuracy of competing accounts of economic growth and the evolution of poverty. For the time being, I want to bracket the questions of whether or not, why and when, poverty declined on a global, historically unprecedented scale. Instead, I want to focus now on the issue that Sullivan and Hickel have pointed to—namely, that it is money that has been used as the measure of development in this discourse, and that non-money activities—while sometimes taken into account—do not typically play a central role in economic analyses of this kind. And when they are included in calculations they are converted into equivalent general-purpose-money terms. In the debate between economic historians on the issue of historical development, a certain conception of money plays a central role. The discourse and debates on devolvement are therefore one more clear example of how the use of money facilitates quantification and comparison across time, even if many scholars are aware of the limitations involved in attempting to view history through this lens.

In spite of the limitations pointed out by Sullivan and Hickel, calculating and quantifying economic development in this way remains a common practice for good reason: It has methodological benefits because of the availability and familiarity of conceptual tools drawn from mainstream economics. Moreover, there is something intuitive about such approaches. Contemporary readers can readily imagine what it might mean to have a purchasing power of less than two dollars a day. It is not obvious what tool, other than money, could be deployed to measure development over time or, conversely, to quantify the lack of development over time.[17]

16 Ibid., 28–9.

17 I am certainly not claiming that arguments about the history of economic growth use only money measures. Of course, it is true that economic historians working on this complex issue have used a wide range of non-money data (population growth, light-usage levels, industrial output, and more) to document the take-off of modern

This obstacle may explain why the history of racism and the scale of inequality between racialized groups is very often presented in monetary terms. In reparations talk, the problem of racism is regularly framed through the concept of the "racial wealth gap." This gap can be measured in dollars and cents. Advocates who present such arguments make use—at least implicitly—of a view of historical development that can be priced. If economic progress is calculated in money terms, then it would stand to reason that the measure of integration of historically marginalized groups into the general trend of history can also be described in the language of money. Conversely, the gap in money wealth and income between groups is taken as an index of the degree of the abiding impact of historical injustices on the lives of contemporaries.

A report on the racial wealth gap produced by the liberal American think tank Brookings illustrates this way of reasoning:

> Centuries of discrimination and exploitation have left Black Americans much poorer than white Americans. The median white household has a net worth 10 times that of the median Black household. If Black households held a share of the national wealth in proportion to their share of the U.S. population, it would amount to $12.68 trillion in household wealth, rather than the actual sum of $2.54 trillion. The total racial wealth gap, therefore, is $10.14 trillion.
>
> There is a vital and vibrant conversation in America today about reparations programs and other expenditure-based approaches to close the racial wealth gap. These investments are a moral imperative and an urgent economic necessity.[18]

---

economies. Meanwhile economic historians are usually well aware of the limits of their methodologies. Morten Jerven, "An Unlevel Playing Field: National Income Estimates and Reciprocal Comparison in Global Economic History," *Journal of Global History* 7, no. 1 (2012): 107–28. My point is simply to highlight the fact that money remains a convenient and widely used measure in academic discussions and popular discussions about wealth in general and that this has important consequences for the way that historical development is understood.

18 Vanessa Williamson, "Closing the Racial Wealth Gap Requires Heavy, Progressive Taxation of Wealth," Brookings, December 9, 2022, brookings.edu. William Darity and A. Kirsten Mullen also argue that reparations for slavery must be aimed at closing the "wealth gap"; "'From Here to Equality' Author Makes a Case, and a Plan, for Reparations," NPR, June 17, 2020, npr.org.

When reparations for slavery are viewed as a policy that can contribute to closing the "racial wealth gap," money is used as the measure of the failure or success of antiracism. To close the "racial wealth gap" would involve including groups who have been disadvantaged through racialization in the general pattern and trend of economic growth. It is a game of catch-up, not dissimilar to the one developing nations are told to play with the Global North.

This would seem a logical way to proceed in a society in which money is so central to daily life and in which economic activity is quantified in dollars. But left-wing critics of reparations—most notably Adolph and Touré Reed and Walter Benn Michaels—take issue with this reasoning, because they note that it does not deal with the underlying problem of economic inequality. Reparations are not designed to decrease inequality—something they say socialists should be interested in—but are concerned only with ensuring that the inequality is equally distributed among people regardless of skin color. How progressive would such a policy really be?

The price of reparations, the profitability of slavery, and the Williams thesis

It bears repeating, because it is so often forgotten, that reparations advocates have proposed a very wide range of policies well beyond the distribution of cash. There is no consensus on what form reparations for slavery should take. Both symbolic and material measures have been discussed. Meanwhile, those calling for money payments have also proposed a variety of mechanisms for dispensing those funds to the broader society. To be sure, many still think that reparations for slavery would necessarily involve "checks in the mail." But proponents of reparations have also proposed that the money should be used to finance scholarships, centers of research, land grants, and government projects, among other things. Indeed, some have proposed using reparations to support noncapitalist forms of social organization such as producer cooperatives.

Regardless of what form they take, however, the price of reparations payments has usually been calculated in money terms. Financial techniques of quantification and comparison across time have also been employed in the process. Any idea of reparations requires thinking the relationship between past, present, and future in terms of money. But because the chronological distance involved is so great, money's usefulness as a temporal instrument appears to be pushed to its limits. There is no agreement about the correct price to be paid as reparations, nor is there any agreement about what should be used as the basis for any such calculation. Existing estimations vary enormously, in part because claimants are asking for payment for different injustices—slavery, colonialism, structural racism, and more—from different beneficiaries. Furthermore, the sums that have been proposed often reflect an attempt to balance different concerns: the estimation of the scale of past injustices in monetary terms on the one hand, and the feasibility that such sums can actually be paid on the other.

It is interesting to review briefly some of the different numbers that have been mentioned. At one extreme, a little-known group called Collectif des filles et fils d'Africains déportés (COFFAD) has demanded that Europe pay the enormous sum of $960 trillion to "Black Peoples":

> The amount that western countries should pay to Black Peoples for having enslaved Africans and used them for forced labor and for having seized (by violence) Africa and its resources since the fifteenthth century. In addition to these reparations, COFFAD urges African states to unilaterally denounce the alleged debts they owe to the west.[19]

Demands like these can easily be dismissed as fanciful. Considering that the World Bank has estimated that global GDP in 2023 was $106.17 trillion, it is unrealistic that the money COFFAD demands could ever be paid.[20] It is hard to believe their claim that this calculation is based on reliable information.[21] But the number reflects an attempt to put a price on hundreds of years of different forms of exploitation, from slavery to

19 "Le Temps de réparations est venu pour les Africains aussi," Collectif des filles et fils d'Africains déportés, January 8, 2000, remy.clarac.free.fr.

20 "GDP (Current US$)," World Bank Group Data, data.worldbank.org.

21 "Based on reliable databases the COFFAD has estimated that the amount owed is over US$960 in current terms (or around 1 quadrillion Euro)." "Le Temps de réparations est venu pour les Africains aussi." .

colonial exploitation and forced labor, and calls for the repudiation of debts. Accounting for all of that would be an incredibly difficult task—if it is at all possible—and would surely amount to a very large amount of money.

This unusual figure is far above what most other activists have called for in the past, however. Not all reparations claims have sought to compensate the entire African continent and Black peoples in general. Most claims have been put forward in a national context. In 1969, James Forman claimed that the much smaller sum of $500 million should be paid, but he was speaking only about the American case. In 1968, the Republic of New Africa (RNA) called for land redistribution and $10,000 "for every black person."[22] Later on, in 1972, the RNA presented its so-called Anti-Depression Program to Congress. The program called for the establishment of a new African nation that would reject "laissez-faire capitalism" and instead embrace the cooperative principles of *Ujamma*; a type of socialism that had attracted widespread international attention after Julius Nyerere instituted it as president of Tanzania.[23] In 1974, one of the founders of the RNA, Imari Obadele, claimed that an election among the Black population across thirty counties in Mississippi had mandated him to

> seek from the United States government two reparations programs. The first is a $200 million Deep South pilot project to fund 20 New Communities with co-op industries and farms. The other is a comprehensive project which would use $57.6 billion over two years to fund 4,000 New communities in the Deep South, give some cold cash to every black family, and place $1 billion, without strings, into the hands of black groups around America to improve the quality of life in existing black communities.[24]

22 "The Republic of New Africa: Declaration of Independence—1968," in Michael T. Martin and Marilyn Yaquinto, *Redress for Historical Injustices in the United States: On Reparations for Slavery, Jim Crow, and Their Legacies* (Durham, NC: Duke University Press, 2007), 588.

23 See "The Anti-Depression Program of the Republic of New Africa," reprinted in William Van Deburg, *Modern Black Nationalism: From Garvey to Louis Farrakhan* (New York: NYU Press, 1997), 197.

24 Imari Abubakari Obadele, "Speaking Out: On the Matter of Black Survival," *Ebony*, May 1974, 84.

In 1994, when Mark Berry sued the US government, he based his argument on General Sherman's promise of forty acres and a mule. He asked for forty acres of government land in San Francisco or $3 million in damages. The plaintiff, who represented himself in court, argued that the Freedmen's Bureau Act entitled him to the forty acres of land, but he was willing to accept payment in cash as a compromise. The judge dismissed the case on procedural grounds and did not consider it on the merits. He decided that the court did not have jurisdiction in this matter and did point out that the statute of limitations had passed six years after the Freedmen's Bureau Act. He added that, in any case, said act would have entitled Berry to land in "insurrectionary states," in other words the old South and not in San Francisco.[25] In 1995, the US government was sued for kidnapping and enslavement in *Cato v. United States.* For this the plaintiffs asked for $100 million.[26] In short, the sums of money that have been mentioned have varied greatly.

Critics of reparations for slavery regularly ridicule the amounts of money cited by groups like COFFAD. But in some instances, the basis of the calculations is obvious and well founded. When the president of Haiti Jean-Bertrand Aristide requested reparations from France and cited the specific sum of $21,685,135,571.48, he was mocked by the French press.[27] But this number was based on the indemnity that Haiti was forced to pay France for their independence and as reparations to French slave owners for the financial losses they incurred. Many years after Aristide was forced out by a coup d'état, the *New York Times* published a report that supported his claims and calculations. The amount could be calculated so exactly because it was linked to reparations payments that Haiti already paid out.

If COFFAD's number seems unreasonably large, the compensation demanded by Haiti could be viewed as a modest amount which leaves out consideration of the economic value produced by slavery. Other former slave colonies have asked imperial metropoles for more money.

25 Roy L. Brooks, "Toward a Perpetrator-Focused Model of Slave Redress," *Berkeley Journal of African American Law and Policy* 6, no. 1 (2004): 53–4.

26 *Cato v. United States*, nos. 94-17102, 94-17104, United States Court of Appeals, Ninth Circuit, December 4, 1995.

27 "Haïti réclame réparation à la France—La drôle de politique de développement d'Aristide," *Le Devoir*, May 17, 2003, ledevoir.com.

It is estimated that Suriname could ask for nothing less than €50 billion from the Kingdom of the Netherlands, for instance.[28] But the wide divergence in amounts of money that have been mentioned illustrate an underlying difficulty in establishing a firm basis for reparations claims. What should be included or excluded from such calculations? This question is extraordinarily complex. But it does not mean that it cannot be done.

The Legacies of British Slavery project based at University College London and the research of historians Nicholas Draper and Catherine Hall revealed the details of the incredible program of reparation that the British government set up to compensate slave owners for their losses at the abolition of slavery.[29] The work of the Slave Compensation Commission demonstrates, among other things, that when the fortunes of slave owners were at stake, the government was able to summon the resources and political will to engage in a massive accounting and tabulation of the price of all the slaves in its domain and distribute sums of money accordingly. The reparations program was a remarkable feat of bureaucratic prowess: It involved estimating the money price of every slave—young and old, man and woman—in different regions of the empire. The amount eventually paid out was equivalent to 40 percent of British government expenditure.[30] The payments were still being made well into the twentieth century. In a documentary on this issue, the historian David Olusoga described this as a government bailout of slave owners, drawing a parallel with the government bailouts that followed the financial crisis of 2008. Reparations activists have taken note of the insights that the work of the UCL historians has provided and the calculations that were carried out by the Slave Compensation Commission.

The need to establish a firm basis for reparations claims has coincided with a renewed interest on the part of historians in the question of the economic impact of Atlantic slavery and its relation to capitalism. But there is no consensus among researchers about the profitability of slavery and the slave trade in the Atlantic world, and

28 "Cariben eisen vergoeding slavernij," NOS, March 10, 2014, nos.nl.

29 Catherine Hall et al., *Legacies of British Slave-Ownership: Colonial Slavery and the Formation of Victorian Britain* (Cambridge: Cambridge University Press, 2014).

30 Catherine Hall, "Britain's Massive Debt to Slavery," *Guardian*, February 27, 2013, theguardian.com.

its relative weight vis-à-vis the rest of the economy. The scholarly arguments on these issues have been multifaceted and are bound up in even larger—and perhaps even more controversial—debates about the reasons for the so-called rise of the West or the "great divergence" between Europe and "the rest." Many of the discussions have centered on Eric Williams's arguments in *Capitalism and Slavery*, in which he made a number of strong claims, among them that the profits from slave labor in the British colonies were so significant that they provided the capital necessary to spur the Industrial Revolution. The Williams thesis has understandably received new interest in light of calls for reparations.[31]

No one doubts that slavery was an important economic activity in the Atlantic world. But historians' views on the issues just outlined depend a great deal on the way in which they measure and define the economic value produced by slavery and its relative impact alongside other activities. It is not a simple matter to quantify these things, especially when historical data is not always available. Unsurprisingly, the historiographical debate on this issue has revolved around methodological choices. Some have argued that one should look at the profits from the slave-trading voyages as the most reliable figures on the impact of the slave trade. Since the category of profit existed at the time (unlike the concept of GDP, for example) focusing on this data has certain methodological advantages. Even so, determining what constitutes an accounting profit for the purposes of historical research—and how profit can be considered historically—has been a bone of contention in the broader field of economic history.[32] Other historians have argued that focusing narrowly on the profits of slave-trading voyages or even of plantation agriculture leaves out a great deal of economic activity that was affected by the activities of enslaved labor, and the triangular trade of which it formed part.[33]

31 *Capitalism and Slavery* was recently reprinted as a Penguin Classic. Eric Williams, *Capitalism and Slavery* (London: Penguin, 2022).

32 Mary O'Sullivan, "The Intelligent Woman's Guide to Capitalism," *Enterprise and Society* 19, no. 4 (2018): 765.

33 Joseph Inikori has, for instance, argued that Africa also provided an essential market for manufactures from the Atlantic economy and that this provided a crucial demand stimulus for economic development in Europe. Joseph Inikori, *Africans and the Industrial Revolution in England: A Study in International Trade and Economic Development* (Cambridge: Cambridge University Press, 2002).

I cannot review the very large scholarship on the economic impact of Atlantic slavery on European economies in this chapter. But I would like to note that there is a tendency across this literature to attempt to quantify these activities in money terms using methods drawn from contemporary economic theory. Measures like value added or GDP are applied, somewhat anachronistically (but perhaps, usefully), to past epochs during which national accounting statistics were lacking. [34]

Focusing on Britain, David Eltis and Stanley Engerman used a value-added approach to estimate the importance of sugar-related industries in the eighteenth century versus other industries and argue that returns from slavery were not higher than in other sectors. They found that "if the value added and strategic linkages of the sugar industry are compared to those of other British industries, it is apparent that sugar cultivation and the slave trade were not particularly large, nor did they have stronger growth-inducing ties with the rest of the British economy."[35] Wool manufacture and iron making may have been more important. However, more recently, Klas Rönnbäck has used a similar value-added approach to estimate the importance of the value chains of sugar-, cotton-, and tobacco-related industries as a percent of total value added in the British economy. In contrast to other studies, he finds that:

> If we add the activities in the American plantation complex [to the British part in the triangular trade, which he calculates as about 5 percent of British GDP by the late eighteenth century], as well as the industries in Britain directly dependent upon this (either for inputs of raw materials or for markets for output), the estimated figures show that economic activities equivalent to around 11% of British GDP were directly involved in or associated with the Triangular Trade and the American plantation complex. Activities of this

34 This is not intended as a general criticism of such approaches. I am simply noting that the methods used—which have undoubtedly advanced knowledge of the scale of the economic impact of slavery—involve the retrospective application of contemporary economic categories of analysis to a time period during which these same categories did not exist as categories of practice. In that sense they are anachronistic.

35 David Eltis and Stanley Engerman, "The Importance of Slavery and the Slave Trade to Industrializing Britain," *Journal of Economic History* 60, no. 1 (2000): 123.

> magnitude can hardly be dismissed as marginal to the British economy at the time.[36]

These contrasting studies show that even when the similar methodologies are employed, results can differ.

Even if it is clear that economic impact from slavery was substantial, it is another matter to determine if, or to what extent, it caused or sparked industrial innovation. While most scholars are skeptical of monocausal accounts of the Industrial Revolution, it seems clear that slavery played an important role in these developments. But was it a decisive factor? Those who think it was not have posed the question why it is that Britain industrialized while other slave-trading countries did not. Consider the cases of Portugal or the Netherlands, for example; both participated significantly in the slave trade and both industrialized relatively late. The link between slavery and the rise of industrial capitalism cannot, therefore, be so straightforward.

A recent debate among historians about the impact of the slave trade in the Netherlands is a very interesting case to consider because it deals with many of these questions head on. The issue of the importance of slavery for the Dutch economy, which had been discussed before, reemerged when Karwan Fatah-Black and Matthias van Rossum argued that existing attempts to estimate the economic impact had focused too narrowly on profits. They used another method, which they called a "gross margin" approach, on the grounds that it would permit a consideration of the effects of the slaving business on the broader economy. The transport of slaves also provided what the authors call a "catalyst effect" to other industries, such as shipbuilding, and the authors also drew attention to the stimulus that the triangular trade provided for the production of consumer goods more generally.[37] These young scholars were criticized by historians from an older generation, however, who attacked the "gross margin" methodology as being tantamount to suggesting that slave trading incurred no costs. The critics, among

36 Klas Rönnbäck, "On the Economic Importance of the Slave Plantation Complex to the British Economy During the Eighteenth Century: A Value-Added Approach," *Journal of Global History* 13 (2018): 327.

37 Karwan Fatah-Black and Matthias van Rossum, "Beyond Profitability: The Dutch Transatlantic Slave Trade and Its Economic Impact," *Slavery and Abolition* 36, no. 1 (2015): 67–8.

them David Eltis and the Dutch historian Piet Emmer, argued that focusing on the profitability of the slave-trading companies is a better approach. They demonstrated that one important Dutch slaving company, the Middelburgsche Commercie Compagnie (Middelburg Commercial Company), had comparatively low profit margins. Thus, they maintain that, contrary to what many suppose, the profits from the slave trade were not as significant a part of the Dutch economy, and that other trades, such as whaling, were more lucrative by comparison.[38] As whaling and herring fishing would have also provided a stimulus effect on shipbuilding, for example, they ask why the focus is exclusively on slavery.

This debate was taken up and given a new twist when Ulbe Bosma and Pepijn Brandon attempted to estimate the impact of the Atlantic slave-based activities on the Dutch economy in the half century between 1750 and 1800. This required looking not only at the slave trade but at the impact of goods that enslaved labor produced, like sugar, coffee, and tobacco. Transportation by Dutch ships was also taken into account, as they commonly carried goods produced in French slave colonies to other areas of Europe, such as the Baltic. These scholars used the measure of gross domestic product. They estimate that slave-labor-based activities accounted for 5.2 percent of the economy of the Dutch Republic, 10 percent of the richest province, Holland, was based on slavery, and 19 percent of Dutch imports and exports was made up of goods produced by slaves in the Atlantic region in the year 1770, which was a high point of this economic activity. Slavery can thus be said to have been a highly significant factor in Dutch wealth.

The differences between these historians reflect the fact that all attempts at economic quantification of slavery are beset by problems of what Brandon calls "demarcation." In addition to the problem of trying to study a transnational economic process through a national framework, "there is the far from easy matter of how to delineate costs and benefits in the slave trade and the slave-based commodity trade."[39] Finally there is the issue of determining what economic

38 David Eltis, Pieter C. Emmer, and Frank D. Lewis, "More Than Profits? The Contribution of the Slave Trade to the Dutch Economy: Assessing Fatah-Black and Van Rossum," *Slavery and Abolition* 37, no. 4 (2016): 724–35.

39 Pepijn Brandon, "The Value of Figures," *Slavery and Abolition* 42, no. 1 (2021): 159.

activities can be said to be linked to slavery: "Economic activities aimed at or derived from the Atlantic plantation complex become hard to separate from those that were not."[40] Together with Fatah-Black and Van Rossum, Bosma and Brandon demonstrate the importance of widening the focus of economic studies of slavery to take into account a broader range of activities. They also draw attention to the difficulties involved in dealing with such questions from a strictly national perspective. For Eltis, Engerman, and Emmer, the lines of demarcation must be drawn more narrowly however, if accurate figures are to be arrived at.

All the studies mentioned above attempt to measure the economic impact using money. But Atlantic slavery also influenced the culture and practices of the early modern and modern worlds in ways that may have spurred economic growth but that are difficult to quantify. Historians working on the case of the United States have drawn attention to the management, financial, and accounting techniques developed on plantations, noting that these innovations also proved to be crucial stimuli for the development of modern capitalism.[41]

Where would one even attempt to start enumerating the immense effects of the Atlantic exchange on the realm of culture and the world of ideas? Taking stock of the deep reservoirs of cultural production and innovation in what Paul Gilroy dubbed the Black Atlantic would seem an impossible task. It is difficult enough to track the contributions that enslaved labor made to leading cultural institutions. Over the last two decades, a number of universities have taken it upon themselves to investigate their own historical links to slavery. Brown University in the United States set the trend in this regard, but others have followed suit. In general, these institutional studies have shown that money from slavery played a significant role in the history of these prestigious centers of learning. Initiatives like these have also produced calls of reparations. Georgetown has recently set up a "reconciliation" fund that "awards $400,000 annually to community-based projects that aim to have an

40 Ibid., 160.

41 Ibid., 162. Sven Beckert and Seth Rockman, *Slavery's Capitalism: A New History of American Economic Development* (Philadelphia: University of Pennsylvania Press, 2016).

impact on Descendant communities whose ancestors were once enslaved on Maryland Jesuit plantations."[42] Is this enough?

It is not clear how Georgetown arrived at the figure of $400,000, but they will have faced the similar problems encountered by others who have attempted to put a price on reparations claims. Even if the historical question of the past economic impact of slavery could somehow be settled, the difficult issue of explaining how this value should be passed down to the present would present another equally complex problem. One way this issue has been tackled in the past has involved using the framework of the time value of money in an attempt to calculate the "present value" of enslaved labor. This is not an easy operation, and it raises a number of difficult questions: Should slave labor be assimilated, for the purposes of quantification, to wage labor? Should the "asset values" that enslaved people represented be taken into account, as in the case of the Slavery Compensation Commission? And what has been the abiding economic impact of these factors over the intervening period from the formal abolition of slavery until today? In other words, what price should be paid for all the years that descendants of the enslaved were deprived of the opportunity to dispose of the money that the labor of their ancestors produced?

What rate of interest should be applied when calculating the price of reparations payments today? Compounding interest could yield massive sums. Thomas Craemer, for example, has calculated scenarios in which a 1 percent change in the interest rate could produce a present value of reparations that fluctuates from as much as half of the GDP of the United States at the time of calculation to six times GDP.[43] Reparations claims on such a large scale might be impossible to pay. Pragmatic matters need to be taken into consideration as well.

But this is just the tip of the iceberg in terms of practical problems involved in any attempt to price reparations using the techniques of modern finance. Political philosopher Robert Meister has pointed out several issues that have often been overlooked in the discussions so far. Among his most interesting observations are three simple

42 "Reconciliation Fund," Georgetown University, georgetown.edu.

43 He also says that the reparations payments which France exacted from Haiti were based on an estimation of ten times the annual wealth of Haiti. Thomas Craemer, "Estimating Slavery Reparations: Present Value Comparisons of Historical Multigenerational Reparations Policies," *Social Science Quarterly* 96, no. 2 (2015): 60.

points: First, that one of the implications of present value calculations of historical injustice along the lines of those described above is that older injustices are rendered more valuable in current terms than more recent crimes by the power of compounding interest.[44] Second, because the wealth of current capitalist societies is held mostly in the form of highly liquid assets, attempts to seize that wealth can always be scuppered by what he calls the "suicide bombers of Wall Street," who showed in 2008 that they were willing to let the entire financial system self-destruct unless the state intervened to preserve their wealth. In other words, Meister suggests that the attempt to exact financial retribution for historical injustice runs the risk of provoking capital to destroy the accumulated wealth of society rather than to disgorge it. Third, that the state has consistently acted to preserve unjustly accumulated wealth by acting as a guarantor of the liquidity of the financial system through institutions such as central banks, which backstop financial markets, and through government bailouts. As such, the state is also complicit in perpetuating the original injustice by acting to preserve the financial gains that accrued from it.

But in this last point, Meister sees an opportunity that can be exploited for progressive purposes. He claims that recognizing the implicit liquidity guarantee provided by the state could open the way to a project of historical justice that uses this to its own advantage. Meister, who says he is writing in the spirit of Marxian political economy, suggests that in order to conceive of justice in the era of financialized capitalism, we must penetrate and adopt the hegemonic language of finance.[45] He proposes to turn the technologies of modern finance against those who hold financial power by conceiving of justice as a financial derivative; more specifically as an *option*. In a highly original move, Meister introduces the options pricing theory of Fischer Black and Myron Scholes to the question of historical injustice. Instead of thinking of historical justice in terms of a debt that must be repaid at some moment, Meister suggests that it can be conceived of as an option that could be priced and

44 Makerere Institute of Social Research MISR, "A Democratic Theory of Finance for the 21st Century. Prof Robert Meister," YouTube, July 14, 2020, youtube.com.

45 Robert Meister, *Justice Is an Option: A Democratic Theory of Finance for the Twenty-First Century* (Chicago: University of Chicago Press, 2021), 10.

rolled over. This optionality would provide strategic benefits for progressive forces.

What are the advantages of such an unorthodox approach to historical justice? Most importantly, Meister believes that it would circumvent the threat of a capital strike that would likely ensue in any revolutionary event during which justice would be demanded. In other words, it would prevent the suicide bombers from blowing up the financial system altogether. This is partly because pricing justice as an option would mean that the money would not have to be paid out all at one moment. A moment in which the price for justice would be paid out in full would be tantamount to a revolutionary situation, Meister notes—one that is likely to be stymied by powerful interests. If the sum of money were to be paid out all at once, then modern capitalism would cease to function. Meister suggests an alternative: Historical injustice could be conceived of as a "long put" option for which no "premium" has been paid. If the possibility of an eventual revolutionary moment during which the wealth that resulted from said injustice would have to be redistributed might be calculated as an option, to be exercised *or not*, then it could also be priced by options theory. In this way, a premium for staving off revolution, for rolling over the option, could be exacted. This premium could be used to fund all sorts of progressive policies. He suggests that we can use existing financial technologies to "design vehicles [for] redirecting the flow of funds, collateral, and risk that could operationalize and implement historical justice as a project for harvesting the ongoing benefits that arise from injustice in the past."[46] Furthermore, since the price of the option would reflect the measure of volatility, at times when revolutionary pressures would be more acute and when the detrimental effects of past injustice are experienced as most burdensome, the value of the option would increase. Thus, delaying the revolutionary moment can yield economic benefits in the short term as the beneficiaries of past injustice are obliged to pay for the insurance that the whole system is not overthrown.

Meister's admittedly highly creative approach to historical justice may strike many readers—as it does this author—as being infeasible. He might respond to our concerns, however, by pointing out that his

46 Ibid., 111.

idea that financial markets should enter into an option contract which would reflect the value of the government's implicit liquidity guarantee mirrors a proposal already made by leading macro-financial thinkers in the wake of the 2008 financial crisis. Meister draws inspiration from economists such as Robert C. Merton, who calculated how much the liquidity guarantee provided by the United States in 2008 would have been worth had it been priced as an option.[47] In other words, it is possible to calculate the price of the insurance policy that the financial system would have to pay the state for stepping in to prevent its systemic collapse. At the moment, such a guarantee is implicitly given, without a premium being charged for it. Meister believes that a democratic theory of finance could find a way to charge such a premium and use the proceeds to fund beneficial programs.[48] The public would be "credited with a new financial asset matching the value of the private financial risk the public has assumed."[49] When everything receives a price the capitalist system is tied up in its own shoelaces, so to speak.

Still, Meister's proposal is unlikely to please those who argue that the injustices of the past—like slavery—cannot be priced. It would involve not only the calculation of past injustice in money terms but also the continual pricing of the "risk" that reparations would have to be paid in full. Instead of seeking to shield domains from the crude quantifying rationale of money, he takes that logic to its extreme.

The consummate automatic fetish: Fictitious capital and derivatives

Meister wants to argue that the measures he is proposing will allow those harmed by historical injustices to share in the economic wealth of society.[50] In this way, he follows reasoning similar to that of Thomas Craemer of the Brookings Institution and activists who view reparations for slavery as a way to close the racial wealth gap. Craemer and

47 Ibid., 116.
48 Ibid., 115.
49 Ibid., 133.
50 Ibid., 110.

Meister both adopt approaches to calculating the price of claims for compensation that draw on the mainstream idiom of financial accounting which, although it is not explicitly stated, in turn uses a notion of general-purpose money that can, among other things, compare values across time. There are good reasons to take such an approach: These are the most obvious tools to reach for when discussing economic and financial matters and they are recognized by the institutions in which claims for reparations have been formulated. But calculating the price of reparations claims in this manner also involves certain assumptions and implications which are morally dubious and economically conservative in ways that would seem to contradict what some might hold to be the radical intent of reparations proposals. While it is indeed essential that any "emancipatory" movement worth the name penetrate what Meister calls the "hegemonic" language of finance, it does not follow that it should also adopt that language as its own. To take on the language of contemporary finance is to view economics from the perspective of capital. But it is precisely this perspective on economic activity and value that has facilitated the historical exploitation and expropriation of humans all over the world. Slavery, and other forms of exploitation, are facilitated by a language of accounting that focuses on economic profit while simultaneously obfuscating its origins in labor.

If they are to penetrate the hegemonic language of finance, it is vital for emancipatory movements to expose the social relations which allow money to function. This is precisely what David McNally attempts to do in his book *Blood and Money*. It begins with an evocative example from ancient Roman history, in which Cicero, writing to a friend, states that he sees 120,000 *sesterces* before him when, in fact, he is describing the slaves he sees standing on the platform. This anecdote illustrates an extreme example of how taking the "money view" can metonymically transform human relations into units of account.[51]

Pecuniary quantification is never neutral. Accounting is better understood as a discursive practice that reflects and perpetuates the interests of contemporary capitalist corporations. Tony Tinker has warned that current accounting practices play a direct role in perpetuating alienation,

51 David McNally, *Blood and Money: War, Slavery, Finance, and Empire* (Chicago: Haymarket, 2020), 26, ebook.

and scholars working in the field of critical accounting studies have emphasized the importance of developing different "emancipatory" forms of accounting.[52]

One of the tasks of emancipatory projects has been to articulate another perspective on the dominant system of economic relations which foregrounds its rootedness in exploitation and expropriation. The most developed of these critical traditions is undoubtedly the Marxian one. Marx's project in *Capital* was to provide a critique of bourgeois political economy. In the first volume, this critique required Marx to penetrate the "dazzling" money form to examine the sources of *value* in the exploitation of labor.[53] Concepts such as value and the organic composition of capital are tools that are intended to facilitate a radical accounting of capitalism. It seems only logical that these tools could be better suited to any attempt at quantifying the exploitation of slave labor than the metrics of bourgeois economics.

Given Meister's stated commitment to the spirit of Marxian critique, it is surprising that his theorization of justice as an option seems systematically to confuse price and value. Or perhaps it is fairer to say that it does not engage with value, in the Marxian sense, in a substantial and direct way. In an article that appeared before the publication of *Justice Is an Option*, Meister puts the issue of value aside when he references the so-called transformation problem—something I will discuss in more detail below—and suggests that it does not apply to liquidity.[54] In *Justice Is an Option*, on the other hand, Meister's engagement with Marxian economics consists primarily in suggesting that the concept of

52 Sonja Galhoffer and Jim Haslam, "Some Reflections on the Construct of Emancipatory Accounting: Shifting Meaning and the Possibilities of a New Pragmatism," *Critical Perspectives on Accounting* 63 (2019): 3. See also Laurie Mook, "Social Accounting for the Social Economy," in Laurie Mook, ed., *Social Accounting for the Social Economy* (Toronto: University of Toronto Press, 2013), 6.

53 Karl Marx, *Capital: A Critique of Political Economy*, vol. 1, trans. Ben Fowkes (London: Penguin, 1991), 139.

54 "The relation between liquidity and value is mediated by market prices, eliminating the need to 'transform' price into value." Robert Meister, "Reinventing Marx for an Age of Finance," *Postmodern Culture* 27, no. 2 (2017). This statement is puzzling since it appears to misconstrue the root of the so-called transformation problem. That problem arises precisely because market prices deviate from underlying labor values. This divergence is exposed by the analysis of the equalization of the rate of profit.

fictitious capital is not a useful one when it comes to an analysis of financial derivatives.[55]

> Capital accumulated in a purely financial rather than material form is thus not usefully described as fictitious to the extent that the options it embodies can be valued—even and especially when what is being valued consists of an enhanced capacity to preserve and expand preexisting value, and this to perform the specific function of vehicles of accumulation.[56]

But, here, Meister's critique seems to rest on a misunderstanding of what is fictitious about fictitious capital. It is *not* the immateriality of financial instruments that make them fictitious capital. Indeed, materiality is hardly the issue, because value itself is immaterial even while it remains objective for Marx. Rather, the fiction lies in the relation between this form of capital and value. Fictitious capital is a claim on future value that has not yet been realized. Of course, many derivatives and futures contracts were designed, at least in the first instance, as an insurance on the realization of future value. Yet the future realization of value still plays an essential role. When this valorization fails to take place, the money value (price) of fictitious capital vanishes. Cédric Durand explains the implications of fictitious capital for the current financialized global economy:

> The liquidity that the financial markets work to organize has the objective of ensuring that the bets investors make on the future valorization process can constantly be transformed into immediately available value. However, this ambition runs up against a "fallacy of composition." Even if each individual actor can offload the securities he holds, that cannot be true of all investors all at once. Keynes clearly demonstrated this point, stating that "there is no such thing as liquidity of investment for the community as a whole. There is a simple explanation for this: the productive capital that has been invested, and the relations of indebtedness that underlie financial securities, do not represent immediately

55 Meister, *Justice Is an Option*, 2.
56 Ibid.

> available value. They are promises. So it is only possible for them to sell if someone else agrees to take them over.[57]

This suggests that Meister's proposal to reformulate justice as an option—in the literal as opposed to a purely metaphorical sense—will likely raise at least two serious problems, one practical, the other strategic.[58] The practical problem is how to get anyone to agree to take the other side of the justice-option contract. It is difficult enough to convince society as a whole that there is a debt to be paid for slavery; why would those whom Meister calls the beneficiaries of past injustice—by which he seems to mean the capitalist class—recognize the optionality of justice? Presumably, because the holders of wealth would prefer this to a revolution. But history abounds with examples of ways to stave off revolutions without the use of options contracts.

The more serious problem, from the point of view of an emancipatory program, is the strategic one. The implications of embracing the "option form" is the necessary preservation and even intensification of capitalist relations of production and therefore also the amplification and continuation of the exploitation upon which these relations are based. Meister's embrace of options can be seen as a form of commodity fetishism since it ignores the social preconditions and consequences of economic derivatives.

Derivates have grown to become an essential part of the functioning of modern capitalism, and Marxian economists have had to take due note of their impact. As Bryan and Rafferty have shown, derivatives can be understood, from the point of view of Marxian economics, as an advanced form of money.[59] One of the functions of the money

57 Cédric Durand, *Fictitious Capital: How Finance Is Appropriating Our Future*, trans. David Broder (London: Verso, 2017), 42.

58 "By showing ways to price historical justice *as* an option, this chapter takes up the task of showing why my claim that justice *is* an option is more than a metaphor," Meister, *Justice Is an Option*, 109.

59 "Derivatives are a new sort of money, directly appropriate to the specific conditions of capital accumulation in the current period. With derivatives, money itself comes to be the embodiment of capitalist competition because derivatives embody, in their composition, the competitive computation of relative values, including conversions across discrete, extant forms of money. So rather than being a passive instrument of competitive processes constituted outside the domain of money, derivatives as money internalise the competitive

commodity in Marx's account is precisely the comparison of disparate commodities. In an era of globalized capitalism and multiple national fiat currencies, derivatives provide a key means of commensurability across time and space.

> The multiple forms of risk-exposure, reflecting the range of possible inter-temporal, inter-spatial, inter-financial-instrument price relativities requires intermediation in a form that is itself flexible and able to reflect the range of possibilities in these relativities. Gold does not meet this requirement, especially in an era when money capital increasingly takes the form of different types of credit money and other financial assets. Derivatives, on the other hand are commodities produced and traded for precisely this purpose.[60]

But, as Bryan and Rafferty make clear, the proliferation of this kind of commodity money has the effect of accelerating and enhancing the dynamic, first identified by Marx, whereby the money form facilitates the production of a homogeneous, socially necessary labor time against which the concrete labor time of individuals is always implicitly measured. This process is experienced by workers and consumers as an ever more burdensome exploitation. The authors argue that the growing use of derivatives are "revealing an intensification of capitalism, with all the contradictions that this entails."[61]

---

process. That gives a new, more dynamic (and ruthless) edge to capitalist competition. Derivatives are, in this sense, distinctly capitalist money, rather than just money within capitalism." Dick Bryan and Michael Rafferty, *Capitalism with Derivatives: A Political Economy of Financial Derivatives, Capital, and Class* (Basingstoke: Palgrave Macmillan, 2006), 137.

60 Ibid., 160.

61 Their explanation is worth citing in full because it so clearly explains why the so-called financialization of capitalism has contributed to the feeling of speed up and time stress that is so widely reported in recent decades. "Our central proposition is that derivatives are intensifying the process of competition between capitals, with direct pressure on labor (as workers and consumers). For any corporation, at any time and any place, derivatives present a real-time measure of asset values. They signal what assets to buy and sell, and at what price. Just as importantly, they reveal to all corporations that there are no longer easy profits to be made by being ahead of the market—the most secure way to increase profits is to get workers to produce more, and for lower costs. Derivatives, we argue are revealing an intensification of capitalism, with all the contradictions that this entails." Ibid., 5.

What is more, the practice of pricing options is always related to a certain estimation of interest rates. Craemer's attempts to calculate reparations for slavery also involve a reflection on what might constitute an acceptable rate of interest. But what are the sources of interest rates? In the fetishistic understanding of the functioning of money, it appears as though money begets more money as a matter of course. Or, as Marx wrote in volume 3 of *Capital*, "it becomes as completely the property of money to create value, to yield interest, as it is the property of pear-trees to bear pears."[62] But, as Durand notes, separating "the valorization process from the production process and the exploitation of labour is a chimera." Indeed, radical approaches to economics are attuned to that fact. So that, while the question of the source of interest rates remains a contested issue, Anwar Shaikh—who has recently expounded a renewed classical approach to economics (one that owes a great deal to Marx)—argues that they are related to the profit rate and are therefore subject to the same "turbulent" process of equalization that results from what he calls "real competition." This competition and drive to realize profits exerts pressures on workers, who are the ones who make the growth of the system possible.[63]

Those who wish to conceive of reparations as a radical transformative project should be attentive to the implications of using the framework and tools of mainstream bourgeois economics and finance. As long as proposals are rooted in a fetishistic understanding of money, their radical potential will remain limited. To be sure, one can make a convincing pragmatic argument for using such an approach in certain cases. But it is worthwhile to explore possible alternative methods of accounting if only to highlight more fully the shortcomings of existing methods. One option would be to start from the perspective of value as opposed to money.

62 Karl Marx, *Capital*, vol. 3, cited in Durand, *Fictitious Capital*, 50.

63 Anwar Shaikh, *Capitalism: Competition, Conflict, Crises* (Oxford: Oxford University Press, 2016), 447.

Accounting for value: Slavery, money, value, and time in Marx

Undertaking a value-based accounting may not seem to be a self-evident choice. For one thing, many notable Marxists might argue that slavery was a noncapitalist mode of production.[64] This view is generally rooted in the understanding that capitalism is associated, fundamentally, with wage labor. Marxists who hold this view are joined by their ideological adversaries on this point. Those who celebrate capitalism sometimes note that it replaced slavery. Such arguments are regularly accompanied by citations drawn from the supposed ideological father of capitalism, Adam Smith, who noted that slavery was an inefficient form of labor by comparison to wage labor. But in making this argument, they often omit to mention the point that Smith was actually making—namely, that a sugar plantation was so profitable that it could support even the inefficient form of labor that was slavery.[65]

Slavery, in the Marxian tradition, has often been associated with the "primitive accumulation" that was necessary for a capitalist dynamic to emerge. But, as Robin Blackburn reminds us, "primitive accumulation" is sometimes misunderstood as being an epoch or phase, when in fact it is better thought of as an ongoing process that also coincided with capitalist accumulation. Slavery has existed for millennia and taken multiple forms, thus making it impossible, in my view, to assign slavery to a single mode of production. Marx himself wrote about a "slave-owning mode of production," but he was also aware of how plantation slavery was transformed by the capitalist dynamic.[66]

---

64 This idea is most famously associated with Eugene Genovese, *The Political Economy of Slavery: Studies in the Economy and Society of the Slave South* (New York: Pantheon Books, 1965).

65 Adam Smith, *The Wealth of Nations* (Chicago: University of Chicago Press, 1976 [1776]), 412.

66 Passages like the following illustrate that Marx was very aware of the different forms slavery can take and the various ways in which extracted surplus appears. "We do not need to go into any further detail here as regards the slave economy (which also passes through a number of gradations from patriarchal slavery predominantly for home use to the plantation system, working for the world market) nor the system in which the landowner cultivates for his own account, possessing all the instruments of production and exploiting labour, whether free or unfree, by deliveries in kind or services paid in money. Here the landowner coincides with the owner of the instruments of production, i.e. with the direct exploiter of workers who are numbered among these elements of production. Rent and profit coincide too—there is no separation of the

A number of scholars have sought to explain that Marx's understanding of slavery was more complex than generally credited by his readers. Pepijn Brandon, for example, points out that Marx himself called attention to the similarities and interrelationships between slave and wage labor in his own writing.[67] John Bellamy Foster, Hannah Holleman, and Brett Clark show that Marx was clearly aware of the fundamental role of plantation slavery, but note that "although slaveowner capitalism clearly existed and had definite historical importance, in Marx's view, it could not constitute the laws of motion of capital as a whole, but rather could only fully develop and prosper on capitalist terms in a context in which wage labor was the predominant form."[68] Nevertheless, their key point and observation is that Marx was well aware of the fact that "free" and enslaved labor were both caught up in the same dance of the valorization of capital. John Clegg argues that market *dependence* is characteristic of capitalism, and because plantation slavery was intended to produce commodities, this fundamental market relation was indeed present. It certainly means, as Clegg shows, that enslaved people produced surplus value, and that their rates of exploitation can be compared to those of wage laborers.

A value-based accounting should show that enslaved labor contributed to the general pool of surplus labor from which all capitals drew. Enslaved people were put to work for the express purpose of producing commodities. Their labor played a direct role in the determination of value as socially necessary abstract labor time.

But is it actually possible to carry out an accounting of this type? The answer, very simply, is that it is not. Even though recent Marxian

---

various forms of surplus value. The entire surplus labor of the workers, which is expressed here in surplus product, is extracted from them directly by the proprietor of all the instruments of production which count among them also the land, and in the original form of slavery even the direct producers themselves. Where the capitalist conception prevails, as on the American plantations, this entire surplus-value is conceived as profit; where the capitalist mode of production does not exist itself, it appears as rent." *Capital*, vol. 3, 940.

67 Pepijn Brandon, "'With the Name Changed, the Story Applies to You!': Connections Between Slavery and 'Free' Labor in the Writings of Marx," in Ulbe Bosma and Karin Hofmeester, eds., *The Lifework of a Labor Historian: Essays in Honor of Marcel van der Linden* (Leiden: Brill, 2018), 47–70.

68 John Bellamy Foster, Hannah Holleman, and Brett Clark, "Marx and Slavery," *Monthly Review*, July 1, 2020, monthlyreview.org.

economics has developed theoretical tools that make value-focused accountings feasible for the current period, the practical challenges involved in any historical calculations would be as significant as those that have plagued conventional approaches, if not more so. Moreover, a value-based approach would suffer from the same moral problem that was articulated by Césaire at the start of this chapter. What I propose to do in the following pages, therefore, is not to carry out an accounting along these lines. My aim is more modest: I would like to explore the outlines of what such a reckoning would involve and how it would differ from the existing attempts to price reparations for slavery. This exercise is still useful, I believe, because it will illustrate the ideological implications of existing attempts at quantifying reparations and reveal how bourgeois conceptions of money underpin a fetishistic understanding of history and temporality.

Outlining the contours of a value-based accounting will yield at least three important results: First, it would show that labor of enslaved people may have had an impact on early modern economies of the Atlantic region in a way that is different from existing analyses in economic history. It would, in short, take a different stance on the issue of what Brandon has called "demarcation." The radius of demarcation would, at once, be enlarged but also blurred because a value-based accounting would necessarily illustrate the mutual imbrication of slavery with other forms of exploitation. From a political perspective, this would point the way to opportunities for solidarity between movements advocating reparations for slavery and other progressive movements. In order to do this, however, the form of accounting I am advocating would have to surpass the limits of an orthodox Marxian analysis to investigate the sources and conditions of possibility of value that lie "outside" capitalism, to use Nancy Fraser's term.[69] Here, the most important insights would be drawn from feminist economics that take into account the enormous sphere of social reproduction. Enslaved people in the past played a key role in social reproduction, and enslaved people today continue to perform this type of labor.

69 Fraser argues that "capitalism's economic subsystem depends on social-reproductive activities external to it, which form one of its background conditions of possibility." Nancy Fraser, "Crisis of Care? On the Social Reproductive Contradictions of Contemporary Capitalism," in Tithi Bhattacharya, ed., *Social Reproduction Theory: Remapping Class, Recentering Oppression* (London: Pluto Press, 2017), 23.

Second, a value-based accounting would facilitate a new understanding of how the wealth created by slavery might persist into the present. Capital, for Marx, is dead labor: Past value is preserved by throwing it into circulation again and again. Value produced in the past is preserved as it changes form in the circuit of capital; or it is destroyed when it cannot be re-valorized. Although this point is not usually dwelled upon in Marxian economics, value theory has fascinating implications for the issue of intergenerational relations, because value, alienated from the laborer, can persist beyond his or her own lifetime. The labor of our ancestors permeates the contemporary world which we inhabit and is congealed in the spaces we navigate daily.

Third—and following from the second point—this radical accounting would produce an image of historical development as being *layered*, as opposed to *linear*. The picture of historical progress that has been painted by mainstream economics—which, as we have seen, is rooted in a fetishistic understanding of money—is one in which the economic epochs of the past are milestones along the long path toward development. A value-based accounting should point out that the accumulated wealth of the contemporary world—in the form of money or other assets—is suspended in a dialectical relationship between past, current, and future labor. If the spiral of capital valorization were to cease, it would all come falling down.

It must be specified at the start, however, that focusing on value does not imply that all links to money can be severed. This would be impossible, since the economic data that is available is listed in prices. Moreover, in Marxian economics, price and value are analytically distinct but dialectically related. The comparison of commodities as exchange values on the market in the language of price involves abstracting from the concrete labor time contained in them. It is in this process that the social character of labor emerges.[70] Simon Mohun explains that

70 Shaikh puts this point clearly: "It is only in exchange that the true social nature of commodity production is made apparent; and precisely because commodity production is undertaken for personal gain, for the money which is to be made, *it is the money-prices of commodities that serve as the immediate regulating mechanism of the system*. Far from being a 'veil,' money constitutes a very important feedback mechanism." Anwar Shaikh, "Marx's Theory of Value and the Transformation Problem," in Jesse Schwartz, ed., *The Subtle Anatomy of Capitalism* (Santa Monica, CA: Goodyear Publishing, 1977), 116 (emphasis in original).

"value-added [and here he is using value in the Marxian sense] in the aggregate is ontologically the same whether it is expressed in hours of socially necessary labor time or in terms of money."[71] This means any attempt to equate units of labor time with units of money will require a "conversion coefficient." This would be the "value of money" expressed in socially necessary labor hours, or the inverse—namely, the monetary equivalent of labor time (MELT) expressed as the price of an hour of abstract labor.[72] It is crucial to stress that this approach would examine the aggregate value in the capitalist economy. More steps would be needed to determine the value added by particular sectors, such as the plantations of the Americas. The historical accounting would be rendered even more complicated by the fact that the monetary equivalent of labor time would have undergone significant fluctuations over the period under study.

To document the MELT in each period, one would have to perform something akin to a transformation procedure in reverse. The famous transformation problem has been interpreted as an issue about explaining prices. But it can also be read backward to explain time. When prices feedback into the next cycle of production, the tendency of the equalization of the rate of profit sends signals to producers. Competition exerts a constant pressure on the working classes, who are subjects to new schemes to enhance productivity. This is experienced as the compression and intensification of the laborers' concrete labor time in relation to abstract labor time.

Mainstream economics, as we have seen, denies any underlying notion of value beyond price. The transformation problem is thought to be the Achilles heel of Marx's theory even though economists since his time have produced numerous convincing resolutions of the transformation problem.[73] In fact, the explanation of the dynamic whereby prices can diverge from underlying values, and value can be redistributed, is actually one of the great strengths of Marxian-inspired economics. That this tells us a great deal about temporality is another.

71 Simon Mohun, "A Celebration of the Labour Theory of Value," Keizai Seminar, October 24, 2017, 7, available at scribd.com.

72 Ibid., 8.

73 For an article that reviews many of the most recent theories, see Simon Mohun and Roberto Veneziani, "Value, Price, and Exploitation: The Logic of the Transformation Problem," *Journal of Economic Surveys* 31, no. 5 (2017): 1387–420.

The observation that prices and values diverge has significant consequences for the historiographical debate about the economic impact of slavery in the Atlantic world. It offers a new perspective on the question that has been so central to the historiographical debates on the economics of slavery—namely, what exactly should be measured. If price and value diverge then measuring the profitability of a single branch of industry can be misleading. This is because, as Marx argued, in the process of exchange, the surplus value produced in one industry can be transferred to another (usually more capital-intensive) industry.[74] Noting that a particular industry has a high profit rate does not necessarily tell us what portion of the aggregate surplus value (produced by society as a whole) is extracted from that particular industry. Value tends to flow from labor-intensive to capital-intensive industries. Unequal exchange can also occur where there are high barriers to competition, and when a particular firm has a very high (if not monopolistic) share of a particular market. Plantation slavery was labor intensive, while iron making—and other industries concentrated in the metropole—may have been capital intensive.[75] As Marx argued, competition between capitals tends to equalize rates of profit across various industries over time. Slave-based agriculture may have initially had high profits, but these may have declined over time.[76] Instead of

74 This is precisely what Marx illustrated in the famous transformation procedure. Moreover, as Brandon notes: "While creating untold misery at the bottom of this system, for the beneficiaries this complicated system created long-distance co-dependencies, principal-agent problems of vast proportions and multiple ways to skim each other's margins that business accounts at best capture only in partial ways. This in essence is what makes the seemingly innocuous question about what constituted profit from slavery far from straightforward in practice." Pepijn Brandon, "The Value of Figures," *Slavery and Abolition* 42, no. 1 (2021): 161.

75 At the same time, it is important to remember that plantation slavery made ample use of technology and was sometimes more capital intensive than other sectors.

76 This would be significant to the other aspect of Eric Williams's thesis which suggested that slavery was abolished because it was becoming unprofitable. This view has been subjected to critique, most famously by Seymour Drescher in *Econocide: British Slavery in the Era of Abolition* (Chapel Hill: University of North Carolina Press, 2010). I am obliged to raise this point as a conditional, however, because it is difficult to know for sure whether the equalization of profit rates across industries would have occurred in the variegated and remote markets of the early modern Atlantic world. I would like to express my gratitude to Pepijn Brandon for sharing his illuminating observations and reflections on this very issue.

asking what profit accrued to plantation owners, for example, it would be a very different matter to determine what the rate of exploitation was in the plantation sector.[77] John Clegg and Duncan Foley have already argued that, in the case of the antebellum US South, "excess surplus value" appropriated in plantations was often taken in the form of rents.[78] From a Marxian perspective, then, it is far from clear that the profits that accrued to the direct exploiters of enslaved people represented a proportionate share of the surplus value that these workers produced. Robin Blackburn has also noted that a Marxian perspective on the study of the historical impact of slavery should reflect upon what he calls the "realization effect" that "plantation demand" provided and which was very significant stimulus to British capital accumulation.[79]

A value-based accounting of slavery should try to determine what percentage of the aggregate value of society was due to enslaved labor. This task is made further complicated by the fact that value is not a transhistorical constant, and so what constitutes abstract value—the price of one hour of abstract labor—in each epoch would fluctuate a great deal. This value, let us recall, is the immaterial but objective reflection of the concrete labor times that have been rendered commensurate through commodity exchange. In an economy where both enslaved and wage labor produced commodities for sale on the same market, value in the abstract would be determined by both these labor processes. In so far as they produced goods for sale in the same market, industries using "free" labor were in competition with industries using enslaved labor. This would have led to the intensification of exploitation—through the maximization of relative and absolute surplus value—in both. What this means is that the increasing exploitation of

77 John J. Clegg has estimated slave exploitation rates for the American South in the early nineteenth century. John J. Clegg, "A Theory of Capitalist Slavery," *Journal of Historical Sociology* 33 (2020): 74–98.

78 "Where slave and wage labor coexist, as in the antebellum USA, the difference between their net products (or surplus value) will regulate capital flows. When slaves produce more surplus value than wage laborers—because slaves may be worked harder or 'paid' less—then slaveowners will be in a position to capture this *excess surplus value* in the form of rent." John Clegg and Duncan Foley, "A Classical-Marxian Model of Antebellum Slavery," *Cambridge Journal of Economics* 43, no. 1 (2018): 2–3.

79 Robin Blackburn, *The Making of New World Slavery: From the Baroque to the Modern, 1492–1800* (London: Verso, 1999), 533.

enslaved people would also have put pressure on wage laborers, and vice versa.[80] Enslaved labor played a role in determining the value of labor power and therefore also had an effect on those waged workers who were forced to compete with slave labor and their rates of exploitation.[81] A value-based accounting of slavery would therefore necessarily reveal that the fate of enslaved and "free" labor were linked. This suggests that slavery may have also had a *negative* impact on "free" workers, since competition locked both in a cycle of increasing rates of exploitation. Reasoning along these lines highlights class solidarities and might contribute to overcoming what some have described as the divisive effects of reparations claims. It would, moreover, show how enslaved and "free" labor co-constituted the time of abstract value and were both subjected to the tyranny of the clock. This is why the increasing penetration of clock-time into the lives of the English working class was paralleled by a similar growth in timepiece ownership and time-based production on plantations, as Mark. M. Smith shows was the case in the American South.[82]

Focusing on value instead of profits has another methodological benefit: It would necessarily lead to an investigation of sources of value outside the labor process. As Anwar Shaikh explains, Marx, following James Steuart, understood that there were, in fact, two sources of aggregate profits in the circuit of capital: The first emerges from the

80 Clegg and Foley, "A Classical-Marxian Model of Antebellum Slavery."

81 The authors make the qualification that "this does not imply that slaves and wage laborers coexisted in a single labor market. Rather, we assume that competition between slave and wage labor took place primarily via capital markets, such that slave prices adjusted to arbitrage differences in the rate of exploitation." Ibid., 3. Robin Blackburn, commenting on the problems with R. B. Sheridan's method of calculating the profits from Britain's Jamaican plantation trade, states that "there are two pitfalls which must be avoided in the use of Sheridan's data. First, his figures include operating costs for the services required by the plantation trade. Second, he includes as 'profits on trade' the profits made by British manufacturers selling to the West Indies; likewise, he includes the profits made by those shipping plantation products. From the standpoint of Marxist political economy such profits did not represent the surplus-value extracted from the slaves but, in the first instance, the surplus-value extracted from the workers and sailors. However, it is a perfectly valid exercise to include such profits under the heading of surplus-value realized as a consequence of plantation demand." Blackburn, *Making of New World Slavery*, 533.

82 Mark M. Smith, *Mastered by the Clock: Time Slavery and Freedom in the American South* (Chapel Hill: University of North Carolina Press, 1997).

exploitation of labor, and the second is the profit from alienation.[83] Slavery was fundamentally linked to other forms of expropriation in ways that were mutually reinforcing. Additional sources of capitalist profit came from alienation and dispossession, thereby drawing the link between slavery, colonialism, enclosure, and theft, and connecting core and peripheries of the expanding capitalist world system. Moreover, as more enslaved people were incorporated into the Atlantic system, the pool of potential labor from which capital could draw would have grown.

Focusing on value would necessarily require one to set the lines of demarcation much more widely than the existing studies on the economic impact of slavery that have focused narrowly on profits. But even this may be too narrow still. Accounting for value remains bound to the money form. It leaves out the vast domain of nonmonetary relations and exploitation. It ignores the enormous sphere of social reproduction that takes place outside the circuit of commodity production, usually in the household. Here, the money form is usually absent. But the labor performed there is essential for all human life to exist, and it underpins the rest of the economy. The domestic labor of women all over the world does not enter into the accounting numbers on profits and losses, but without that labor, profit itself would be impossible because there would be no living labor to exploit. The work of bearing and raising children, of emotional care and nurturing of family members, is an essential precondition for any mode of production, but it is not counted in the conventional language of economics. Historically, these surpluses have been produced and distributed by female hands, not invisible ones. As Mohun and others argue, the value of labor power is not determined in the same way as other commodities on the market precisely because it depends for its reproduction on activity in the social sphere not on the circuit of commodity production. But the productive activities of the enslaved outside of the production of commodities also increased, and subsidizes the pool of value from all of which capitalists could draw. The role of enslaved labor in the sphere of social reproduction is undoubtedly very significant, both historically and today, when countless people are held in captivity to perform domestic labor. And if reparations claims are to

83 Shaikh, *Capitalism: Competition, Conflict, Crises*, 209.

proceed in regions outside of the Atlantic world—the Middle East / West Asia and the Indian Ocean world for example—it will have to reckon with the different forms of slavery and unfree labor that were common in those areas.

Dead labor and the layers of historical development

So far, the approach that I have been explicating has focused solely on the historical impact of slavery. But reparations claims must articulate an economic connection between the past and the present day. We have seen how mainstream approaches achieve this by focusing on the money form and fetishistic understandings of compounding interest. Against this view—in which interest appears as a sort of natural force in need of no explanation—a radical accounting would highlight the intergenerational transfer of value and underline the fact that, in order to preserve and valorize the profits from slavery, capital had to be thrown into circulation again and again and again, subjecting each new generation to further exploitation. For Marx, currently available capital is the result of past labor. His famous line that "capital is dead labour which, vampire-like, lives only by sucking living labour, and lives the more, the more labour it sucks" is more often celebrated as a literary achievement than reflected upon as a statement about how wealth persists over time.[84] Of course, sometimes value is destroyed when profits can no longer be realized and in crises. But there is also a remarkable degree of continuity: One has only to think of the firm Lehman Brothers, which started out as a cotton-trading firm and moved into other industries after the abolition of slavery, to become one of the most important financial institutions in the world in the new millennium—its collapse in 2008 almost brought down the entire financial system. In this sense, some of the wealth that exists today might be conceived of as the labor of previous generations congealed in the form of money and fixed capital. Since, as we have seen, the value produced

84 Marx, *Capital*, vol. 1, 342. McNally describes how in the precapitalist economy of ancient Greece, money played a similar role in conserving past value. "The value of Athenian owls—which created the dominant modular form of money for nearly twenty-five hundred years—was . . . rooted in the past labor of thousands of enslaved people." McNally, *Blood and Money*, 66.

by slavery could very well have been transferred to other industries, and because it is a key proposition in Marxian economics that value changes form, there is no reason to fixate on which particular company had clearly demonstrable links to slavery. The value that enslaved people produced permeated economies.

From the perspective of Marxian economics, therefore, development should be seen not so much as a linear process as a stratified one, as each generation preserves and expands the value produced by previous ones. At first sight, this insight may seem to be contradicted by some of Marx's own writing. After all, he sometimes spoke in the language of "historical development" or of the "degree of civilization" and its role in determining use values.[85] His vocabulary was not dissimilar to the contemporary theorists of linear development that I discussed above when, for example, he stated that "the country that is more developed industrially only shows, to the less developed, the image of its own future." But we should not forget that this level of historical and technological development is the product of past labor.[86] Marx's analysis of the circuit of capital and the valorization process makes clear that the value of the past is preserved but transferred through the production process into new forms (surplus commodities, money profits, etc.). In each new phase of accumulation, the constant capital that is brought together with variable capital in production is the product of past labor.

It is easy to forget that the technologies that surround us, and which are visual evidence of the fact that society which we inhabit is "advanced" are the products of labor. The anthropologist Alf Hornborg has noted that even many Marxists have tended to fall victim to what he calls

85 Take the following passage for example: "On the other hand, the number and extent of his so-called necessary requirements, as also the Manner in which they are satisfied, are themselves products of history, and depend therefore to a great extent on the level of civilization attained by a country; in particular they depend on the conditions in which, and consequently on the habits and expectations with which, the class of free workers has been formed." Marx, *Capital*, vol. 1, 275.

86 As Marx writes: "Nature does not produce on the one hand owners of money or commodities, and on the other hand men possessing nothing but their own labour-power. This relation has no basis in natural history, nor does it have a social basis common to all periods of human history. It is clearly the result of a past historical development, the product of many economic revolutions, of the extinction of a whole series of older forms of social production." Ibid., 273.

"technology fetishism." It is common to enthusiastically embrace the growth of technological innovation because it is understood that these technologies save time and spatial resources. But Hornborg argues, very convincingly, that technology should, rather, be understood as a transfer and condensation of time and resources from the peripheries (in the geographical and social sense) of global capitalism to its core. Technology and money are facilitators of a system of asymmetric exchange. Here, again, it is general-purpose money that plays a central role in displacing and redistributing time:

> Ultimately, all commoditization, and the new forms of asymmetric exchange associated with industrialization, are generated by the very idea of general-purpose money. In the same sense that a biological organism is the manifestation of its metabolic exchanges with its environment, the technological infrastructure of industrial society is the tangible manifestation of global relations of resource exchange, but orchestrated by money. Money and technology are thus recursively and inextricably intertwined. To approach "economic growth" and "technological progress" as separable indices of development is a pervasive illusion that continues to obstruct our grasp of contemporary concerns regarding global justice, sustainability, and financial resilience.[87]

In *Nature, Society, and Justice in the Anthropocene*, Hornborg argues that "artifacts"—most notably technology and, in particular, general-purpose money—have "inertia" to organize social and temporal relations.[88] Money embodies the idea that all things are interchangeable with each other, and this, says Hornborg, "makes it possible to purchase human time as well as entire ecosystems as human commodities."[89]

Once this is understood, we can see that the view of politics and economics as a process of linear development in which more and more

87 Alf Hornborg, "The Root of All Evil: Money, Markets, and the Prospects of Rewriting the Rules of the Game," in M. Spyridakis, ed., *Market Versus Society* (Cham: Palgrave Macmillan, 2018), 53.

88 Alf Hornborg, *Nature, Society, and Power in the Anthropocene: Unraveling the Money-Energy-Technology Complex* (Cambridge: Cambridge University Press 2019), 2.

89 Ibid., 138.

people are included in economic growth must necessarily run into natural limits. Hornborg criticizes apologists for capital like the New Optimists, including Steven Pinker and Hans Rosling, whose apologetic views on development I mentioned earlier in this chapter. The picture they paint of a linear historical process of economic growth is highly problematic. Rosling's argument that the rest of the world is catching up with the core regions of global capitalism or, at least, following in their tracks, relies on a series of compelling graphs which actually conceal a great deal:

> What Rosling misses is that those seven puppets animating his diagrams and presentations, each representing one billion people, don't just stand in line but have societal relations to each other. They are parts of the same global system, and . . . there *are* contradictions and power relations in that system. The low wages of levels 2 and 3 are what make it possible for people at level 4 to buy a car—and why there are no cars on levels 2 and 3.[90]

Hornborg thus makes a point similar to the one I have been arguing for throughout this chapter—namely, that the linear view of history and economic development is a form of fetishism that obscures the social relations that make growth possible. The societal relations that he refers to in the citation above are diachronic as well as synchronic. This is why the idea of development in which everyone can obtain the wealth of the top is shown to be infeasible.

Those who present reparations as a way to close the "racial wealth gap" appear to be caught in the same paradigm as Rosling, Pinker, and the like. Closing said gap may not involve reducing economic inequality more generally. This is because such a redistribution would maintain the exploitative social relations that underpin the resources being transferred and give them value in the Marxian sense. A radical accounting in value terms that exposes the social relations that underpin general-purpose money—that demystifies the fetishism around money—also shows the implications of conceiving of reparations in money terms are more complex and less radical than they may seem.

90 Ibid., 250.

History is not a singular unitary process in which marginalized groups can be excluded or included. Instead, the ever-expanding and progressive time of money capital is revealed to be a bourgeois temporality that lies on top of sedimented layers of exploited human labor. An accounting that decenters the money view and shows the sources of profit in value and in the labor of generations of exploited peoples, necessarily connects these to the lived time of individuals, because value, in the Marxian sense, is a form of temporality. Under capitalism, this temporality is experienced as one of increasing time compression and stress in the lives of workers as rates of exploitation respond to ever greater competitive pressures. Derivatives markets, algorithmic trading, just-in-time production, and managerial techniques, along with new digital technologies and global connectivity, have all contributed to accelerating these tendencies and leading to an experience of what David Harvey has called time-space compression.[91] For some, this progress appears as a force of nature: But it is the circular time of the laboring majority—of repetitive production and debt repayment—that makes the exponential time of bourgeois progress possible.

The homogenization of historical time: Money's function as an instrument of temporality

Emile Durkheim said that it "is the rhythm of social life which is at the basis of the category of time."[92] In the contemporary world it is the circuit of capital that sets the beat. Money plays a central role in this process. General-purpose money is a temporal instrument. If modern temporality is empty and homogeneous it is because money has rendered time fungible. In market exchanges mediated by money, the concrete labor times of individuals are rendered commensurate, and an abstract yet objective socially necessary time emerges. The generalized production of commodities for sale on the market has had the effect of

91 David Harvey, *The Condition of Postmodernity: An Enquiry into the Origins of Cultural Change* (Cambridge: Blackwell, 1990).

92 Emile Durkheim, *The Elementary Forms of Religious Life*, trans. Joseph Ward Swain (London: George Allen & Unwin, 1915), Project Gutenberg, November 13, 2012, 440, ebook.

producing an abstract and homogeneous social labor time against which the concrete and local labor times of each individual are always implicitly compared. This is value.

In the discourse of mainstream economics, the relationship between money and value is obscured, and the link between money and time is mystified. This has led to a fetishistic view of historical progress. The tools of modern finance are used to compare historical epochs in money terms without any consideration of the value that lies underneath. The result is a picture of historical progress that appears to curve ever upward. It looks as though some areas of the globe are further along a path of development than others, and that the rest will follow. But the social relations upon which this development depends are not acknowledged. This growth is possible only if the value created by past labor is valorized again and again. It is dependent on the exploitation of labor of each generation.

Pricing reparations for slavery using the conceptual tools of modern finance may have practical benefits. Redistributing money may be a useful and pragmatic policy in the short or middle term. But we must be aware of the ideological implications of using the language of finance. That language presents economic questions from a particular perspective; one that is emphatically not that of those who produce value in society, but rather the language of those who appropriate it. The choice to use this language is practical but odd: The ready availability and widespread recognition and understanding of orthodox economics makes it a more practical choice than heterodox or Marxian theories. It is odd, because part of what is—or should be—calculated in reparations for slavery is the *exploitation* of enslaved people and this would seem to require a means of accounting that takes the perspective of the exploited.

What if activists chose to abandon attempts to price reparations in the language of modern finance and, instead, formulate their claims as a radical accounting focusing on value? Practical and ethical problems would persist. Such an accounting could never do justice to the history of exploitation and suffering. But, as an intellectual exercise, it might illuminate the economic impact of enslaved people historically and show its fundamental imbrication with other forms of exploitation. It should, moreover, make clear that the world we inhabit is one saturated by the value produced by generations past. This past value, to be preserved, must be re-valorized by exploited labor today and tomorrow and into the future.

The calls for reparations for slavery might be the opportunity to consider alternative paths. In fact, as I showed above, this has already been done by reparations activists who have called for funds to be used to promote noncapitalist modes of production. Focusing on value may befit these more radical projects. At the same time, however, the problems which reparations proposal attempt to tackle are far more complex than a purely economic approach can account for. One reason for this is that the oppression which they seek to redress was not based on class alone.

5

Badges and Incidents of Slavery

Children born of marriages between slaves will be slaves and will belong to the master of the slave woman and not to her husband's master, should husband and wife have different masters.
—Article 12 of the "Code Noir"

Is it more than mere coincidence that the proliferation of reparations politics comes on the heels of the collapse of socialism and extensive doubts about the viability of the nation-state? The global spread of reparations demands and the preoccupation with the past to which it bears witness reflect an unmistakable decline of a more explicitly future oriented politics . . . I would argue that the phenomenon is a kind of transitional substitute for the progressive politics associated with the Enlightenment, cut out for an age of diminished political expectations.
—John Torpey, *Making Whole What Has Been Smashed*

Retrospective politics?

John Torpey's book on "reparations politics" remains one of the most influential scholarly works on the topic to date. The argument in *Making Whole What Has Been Smashed* is a simple one: The proliferation of calls for reparations marks the emergence of a new kind of politics which is characterized by a peculiar relationship to time. The point is elegantly encapsulated and summarized in his descriptive phrase "when the future collapses the past rushes in." Reparations politics are a reaction to the abandonment or decline of struggles for socialism, the Civil Rights Movement, and belief in nationalism, which he says were future oriented. Because the future is no longer a source of political inspiration, activists have now turned their energies and focus onto the past. For Torpey, then, reparations are a form of retrospective politics promoted by "memory entrepreneurs."[1]

It is easy to see why this argument has provoked discussion. It highlights what many observers find most striking about reparations claims—namely, that what is at issue is the rectification of an injustice that took place generations ago. Torpey's work has the virtues of clarity and simplicity but, at the same time, retains an aura of theoretical profundity by alluding to the thought of Walter Benjamin. The title refers to a passage in the *Theses on Philosophy of History* describing Paul Klee's 1920 *Angelus Novus* as an allegory for historical "progress": The angel, in Benjamin's words, appears to want to "awaken the dead and make whole what has been smashed" but is blown away by the winds of progress pushing him backward into the future. Moreover, Torpey's argument relies on a historical periodization that is congruent with earlier explanations of the emergence of "identity politics." These explanations also claimed that a decline of future-oriented ideologies in the second half of the twentieth century can be understood as a cultural turning point that led to new (lesser) forms of political action in which groups seek recognition and other symbolic measures instead of fighting for broad-based or utopian programs. Nancy Fraser, for example, expressed this argument succinctly in the first lines of what has now become one of the most famous essays on the phenomenon of identity politics:

> The "struggle for recognition" is fast becoming the paradigmatic form of political conflict in the late twentieth century. Demands for "recognition of difference" fuel struggles of groups mobilized under the

1 Torpey also says that that the term "memory entrepreneurs" does not necessarily have a negative connotation; John Torpey, *Making Whole What Has Been Smashed: On Reparations Politics* (New Brunswick, NJ: Rutgers University Press, 2017), 19–20. He notes that the idea is associated with Black nationalist groups, ibid., 126.

> banners of nationality, ethnicity, "race," gender, and sexuality. In these "post-socialist" conflicts, group identity supplants class interest as the chief medium of political mobilization. Cultural domination supplants exploitation as the fundamental injustice. And cultural recognition displaces socioeconomic redistribution as the remedy for injustice and the goal of political struggle.[2]

Several years before Tropey, the political theorist Wendy Brown had already explained that political causes like reparations were manifestations of an age of temporal confusion:

> Ours is a present that is hurtled into the future without regard for human attachments, needs, or capacities. A present that dishonors the past by erasing it with unprecedented speed and indifference . . . A present whose inevitable and rapid eclipse is uppermost in the political consciousness of its inhabitants . . . What is there to attach to in a world of such incessant and rapid transformations?[3]

Elaborating on Jacques Derrida's observations that time seems "out of joint," in the contemporary period, Brown argued that

> What conventionally sets time right again is the law; but in Derrida's account, law's traditional connection with vengeance, and even with blood revenge, can do no more than perpetuate the out-of-joint-ness of the times, because it addresses only its symptoms. (This claim would seem to be corroborated by the boundless litigiousness of the present age, and especially by the conversion of historical-political claims of oppression to legal claims for rights or reparations.)[4]

As political theorists were attempting to come to grips with the new temporality that they saw emerging after the "end of history," scholars in a variety of fields became more and more interested in the phenomenon of "collective memory." Indeed, it was common to claim that the

2 Nancy Fraser, "From Redistribution to Recognition: Dilemmas of Justice in a Post-Socialist Age," *New Left Review* 212 (1995): 68.

3 Wendy Brown, *Politics Out of History* (Princeton, NJ: Princeton University Press, 2001), 142.

4 Ibid., 154.

connection between memory culture and identity politics was intrinsic.[5] As I have shown elsewhere, traditional accounts of the rise of collective memory rely on a similar periodization to the one Torpey uses: The leading theorists of the "memory boom" have explained the phenomenon by emplotting it into a story about the general "acceleration of history" in the second half of the twentieth century, and the concomitant abandonment of utopian political projects, and "*grands récits*." In these accounts, memory movements are figured as symptoms of a deeper malaise about the speed of temporality itself.[6] Memory and identity politics have thus been presented as features of the postmodern age—or what François Hartog calls a presentist regime of historicity. "Identitarian" proposals like reparations are thus construed as a panicked and emotive reaction to incomprehensible forces of temporal acceleration, not a serious political strategy.

As one reads beyond Torpey's introduction, however, it becomes apparent that the critique of the temporality of "reparations politics" is aimed primarily at the proposals for reparations for slavery in the United States, rather than at the idea of reparations per se. He reserves his most severe criticism for that specific form of reparations, which he presents as a Black nationalist idea that came to prominence with the decline of the Civil Rights Movement.[7] His temporal argument appears less applicable to the other cases he discusses, and which he also appraises

5 See, for example, Joël Candau, *Mémoire et identité* (Paris: PUF, 1998). Candau also cites historian Jacques Le Goff's distinction between memory and history. Le Goff also sees memory as a manifestation of a later twentieth-century malaise: "Memory is an essential element of what is now called individual or collective identity, the fevered and anxious quest for which is one of the fundamental activities of individuals and societies today." Jacques Le Goff, *Histoire et mémoire* (Paris: Gallimard, 1988), 174 (my translation).

6 Kenan Van de Mieroop, "The 'Age of Commemoration' as a Narrative Construct: A Critique of the Discourse on the Contemporary Crisis of Memory in France," *Rethinking History* 22, no. 2 (2016): 172–91. Reprinted in Kalle Pihlainen, ed., *History in the World* (London: Routledge, 2019).

7 Here, he seems implicitly to rely upon a periodization of the Civil Rights Movement which views it as having been undermined by the rise of "Black power." This account has been criticized by recent scholarship. I discuss some of that literature in more detail in Kenan Van de Mieroop, "The Civil Rights Movement (Re)narrated," in Stefan Berger, Nicola Brauch, and Chris Lorenz, eds., *Analyzing Historical Narratives: On Academic, Popular, and Educational Framings of the Past* (New York: Berghahn, 2021), 209–22.

more favorably. For example, he is rather positive about the American Civil Liberties Act, which compensated Japanese Americans for internment during World War II. The chapter dealing with South Africa discusses a case related to the period of Apartheid, a regime which ended a little more than a decade before he composed the book and can thus hardly be seen as a case of dredging up ancient grievances.

In fact, the body of the book does not elaborate on the temporal argument set out in the introduction in any detail. Instead, it appears that Torpey wishes to address other concerns. In particular, he wants to argue that reparations for slavery, and for the German crimes against the Herero and Nama in Namibia, are not comparable to Holocaust reparations in spite of what many activists working on those cases have claimed. He is obviously keen to respond to what many observers have described as a double standard: Countries, including the US and Germany, among others, have readily supported reparations for the Holocaust but have dismissed reparations in these other cases.

The 1990s and early 2000s—the period immediately prior to the publication of Torpey's book—saw several proposals for slavery reparations rejected. The failure of these cases stood in marked contrast to the victories of Holocaust-related reparations claims in the same decade. The World Jewish Congress was able to reach a $1.25 billion settlement with Swiss banks and relied on the active support of the American government to do so. New York Senator Al D'Amato held a hearing in 1996 on the case in the United States Senate Banking Committee, which he chaired, and President Bill Clinton ordered his deputy secretary of the treasury, Stuart Eizenstat, to investigate the case of Swiss complicity in the Nazi theft of Jewish assets, eventually producing a report which criticized the role of the Swiss as banking for Germany. The former chair of the Federal Reserve, Paul Volcker, led the commission charged with auditing the banks. German companies that were alleged to have profited from slave labor during the Holocaust were also sued during this same period.[8] According to Alfred Brophy, those suits were dismissed by the courts, but shortly afterward, "German companies acting in conjunction with the German government—and under political pressure from New York politicians—agreed to a settlement of something like

8 Christopher Rhoads, "Holocaust Victims Sue German Firms for Profiting on Nazi-Era Slave Labor," *Wall Street Journal*, September 1, 1998.

$5.2 billion."[9] In his role as the special representative of the US president and secretary of state on Holocaust-era issues, Eizenstat would go on to negotiate similar settlements with Austrian companies and the French railways. In short, Holocaust-related claims enjoyed very strong government support, and private companies appeared willing to deal with the issue.[10]

The contrast with slavery reparations proposals was stark. In 2001, the major corporation Aetna was forced to apologize for having insured enslaved people as property of others. Deadria Farmer-Paellmann a law student who publicly exposed the company's historical links to slavery demanded reparations and later filed a lawsuit against a number of companies. Her suit was ultimately unsuccessful.[11] In its reasoning on the case, the court began by recognizing the abhorrent nature of slavery. The judge went on to say that the suit nevertheless failed on numerous grounds. Foremost among the problems with the case, according to the judge, was that the plaintiffs lacked standing; they could not show that they were the victims of slavery. The judge also referred to the statute of limitations. Moreover, he claimed that he was not authorized to make a decision about reparations because of the so-called political question doctrine, which is to say that the issue of reparations was within the remit of the legislative rather than the judiciary branch. During the same period, however, there was little congressional support for any discussion of slavery reparations, even though Representative John Conyers had introduced an act that would set up a commission to study the issue every year since 1989.

Randall Robinson, one of the main figureheads of the reparations movement at that time, was quick to remark on the inconsistent attitudes to Holocaust and slavery reparations claims:

9 Alfred L. Brophy, *Reparations: Pro and Con* (Oxford: Oxford University Press, 2006), 119.

10 Julia Collins, "Taking on the Unfinished Business of the Twentieth Century," *Harvard Law Today*, June 24, 1999. See also "*Nazi Gold*: A Chronology of Events—PBS Frontline," PBS, pbs.org. Under the Biden administration, Eizenstat was once again appointed to the role of special adviser on Holocaust issues by the State Department. "Appointment of Ambassador Stuart E. Eizenstat as Special Adviser on Holocaust Issues," Media Note, Office of the Spokesperson, December 27, 2021, state.gov.

11 *Deadria Farmer-Paellmann v. Fleet Boston Financial Corp. et al.*, United States District Court for the Eastern District of New York, March 26, 2002.

> I was thinking of the rather dramatic contrast here in what happened in the case of the sixteen German corporations that were discovered to have used Jews during the Nazi period as slaves, and the extent to which the U.S. government involved itself in pressing those corporations to make a clean breast of it and to settle with the payment of restitution to the victims and to their heirs. In that case, Stuart Eizenstat was asked by President Clinton to lead the U.S. government effort to press these German corporations to be revealing, as well as to come forward in a settlement offer. It enjoyed the support of both houses of Congress, and, of course, as I've said, the President of the United States, and a settlement was reached for upwards of $5 billion from Volkswagen and other corporations who were found to have been culpable in this area.
>
> It is unrealistic to expect that Aetna, or any other corporation, will investigate itself, make a statement that tells us clearly what its involvement was, without pressure from the outside. And when asked this question, Eizenstat, about the contrast here between our country's efforts on the German corporations and our country's efforts with respect to what Ms. Farmer-Paellmann has worked on, and the general question of reparations, Mr. Eizenstat was not at all forthcoming, nor has been the administration. And it is beyond anyone logically to see the difference in the two cases.[12]

Some wondered if it were possible that the very different reactions to the two reparations cases was evidence of racism. Torpey, for his part, does not think so. Holocaust claims were reasonable, in his estimation, considering the circumstances, and they were well thought out in ways that the other proposals were not. Indeed, Torpey calls the initial 1952 agreement between the Federal Republic of Germany and Israel the "gold standard" of reparations. Although this, and the subsequent Holocaust-related claims of the 1990s, may appear similar to the case of reparations for slavery or German crimes in Namibia, they are in fact very different. What is the difference? Torpey cites three main factors: First, in contrast to slavery reparations or reparations for colonialism, Holocaust reparations were not really about the money (i.e., they were more symbolic measures). Second, they were given to the direct victims

12 "Aetna Acknowledges Issuing Slave Policies During 1850s, Offers Apology, Denies Reparations," *Democracy Now!*, March 14, 2000, democracynow.org.

of the crime in question as opposed to their descendants or other members of a connected group, a point Eizenstat also made, commenting on the same issue.[13] Finally, and most obviously, slavery and the massacre of the Herero and Nama are more remote in time from today than the Holocaust was when a settlement was reached with the Federal Republic of Germany.[14]

To be sure, there are indeed important differences between the cases under discussion, but even with respect to the three points just listed, there are more similarities than Torpey would want to admit: He cites no evidence for the claim that the settlement with the FRG, which saw that government pay out $71 billion by 2013, was not really about the money, as he puts it. Nor is it clear why the requests for compensation for slavery and for the Herero and Nama are so much more manifestly motivated by financial concerns than the former. As a recent book by Daniel Marwecki on the topic demonstrates, the State of Israel—which received much of the compensation—did in fact need the money and material support.[15] Torpey's assertion, that the matter was more one of symbolism, completely omits to mention the very serious controversies that emerged around the symbolic significance of accepting this deal. Public opinion among victims

13 "Calls for Slavery Restitution Getting Louder," *New York Times*, June 4, 2001.

14 He also argues that the Holocaust was of a different scale of severity because the goal was extermination, which was not the case with slavery. He admits stronger parallels between the massacre of the Herero and Nama and the Holocaust, even if he notes important differences: "Unlike in the case of the Jews, however, the Herero took up arms against invaders, though they were substantially outgunned and soon overwhelmed. The Herero suffered the typical fate of those colonized by Europeans in the course of what is known rather euphemistically, as 'European expansion.' In contrast, the Jews were very much a part of the society over which the Nazis assumed control and were butchered simply for what they were rather than for any threat they might have poised to German rule. Moreover, in the case of the Jews no extermination order has ever been found, even if there is no doubt that the genocide against them was sanctioned at the highest levels." Torpey, *Making Whole What Has Been Smashed*, 135–6. It is hard to know where to begin responding to this pitiful reasoning. It sounds as if he is saying that the Herero and Nama are less deserving victims because their fate was typical of colonized peoples and they were not Europeans. Torpey also implies that those who resist violence are less worthy victims. Even if we accept this dubious moral position, Torpey appears to forget that many Jews also participated bravely in armed resistance to Nazi rule, and he seems unaware that Nazi propaganda consistently presented Jews as a threat to the German nation.

15 Daniel Marwecki, *Germany and Israel: Whitewashing and Statebuilding* (Oxford: Oxford University Press, 2020). Ta-Nehisi Coates also explains how Israel benefited from reparations in his "The Case for Reparations," *Atlantic*, May 21, 2014, theatlantic.com.

of the Holocaust was deeply divided about whether to take the money. Moreover, the fact that other groups persecuted by the Nazis, like the Roma and Sinti, and gay people, for example, did not receive any compensation or recognition from the Adenauer government seems to indicate that even the "gold standard" of reparations agreements had serious flaws. Indeed, only those Jews who were connected to the German empire in 1937 were eligible under the 1952 deal, even though most of the victims of the Holocaust came from outside those borders.[16]

Torpey is correct, of course, to state that there were—and still are—individuals alive today who lived through the Holocaust, and individuals who were direct victims of the crime received compensation. This is quite different from the case of reparations for slavery, where those who would stand to receive compensation were not themselves enslaved. But, as Torpey himself points out, proposals to pay reparations to the victims of the Tulsa race riot of 1921 also failed, even though they involved living survivors. Slavery reparations advocates regularly link their claims to more recent injustices, such as the period of legalized segregation, or colonial exploitation and violence. There are numerous individuals who lived through these events. Moreover, compensation for slavery was requested on several occasions in the period after abolition in the nineteenth and early twentieth century by people who had been enslaved. Their calls fell upon deaf ears, however. This has led some legal scholars to argue that the statute of limitations—so frequently invoked to dismiss reparations claims—must be equitably tolled in light of the continuing violations against the descendants of enslaved people.[17]

16 Marwecki, *Germany and Israel*, 20. The symbolic implications of compensating the victims of the Holocaust primarily as "Jews" rather than as any other identity that the victims may have held was not as self-evident a choice as it appears from our perspective today. This may seem an academic point to some, but it has been suggested that many of the victims of the Holocaust also saw themselves as political dissidents persecuted because of their socialist and communist views. The situation was precisely the reverse in the GDR, where victims of the Holocaust were described primarily as "antifascists" even though many of them were persecuted primarily for being Jewish.

17 Robert Westley, "The Accursed Share: Genealogy, Temporality, and the Problem of Value in Black Reparations Discourse," *Representations* 92, no. 1 (2005), 81–116; Eric J. Miller, "Representing the Race: Standing to Sue in Reparations Lawsuits," *Harvard Blackletter Law Journal* 91 (2004); Kaimipono David Wenger, "Causation and Attenuation in the Slavery Reparations Debate," *University of San Francisco Law Review* 40 (2005–6); Suzette M. Malveaux, "Statutes of Limitations: A Policy Analysis in the Context of Reparations Litigation," *George Washington Law Review* 68 (2005–6).

Moreover, Holocaust reparations were also paid to people who were not direct victims. Elazar Barkan notes that one of the difficult issues that had to be dealt with at the time of the original agreement with the FRG was the question of who should receive compensation in the name of heirless victims. The genocide of the Jews wiped out entire families, and the reparations agreement obtained compensation for those without any living successors. For Barkan, part of the novelty of the national claims was that it demanded "the Jewish community as a whole be considered the primary victim and, by moral imperative, the rightful beneficiary of compensation for confiscated heirless and communal Jewish property; and second, that restitution be directed toward the building of a Jewish state." Elazar Barkan describes some of the difficult issues this agreement brought up:

> This unique idea of *national* claims was the most novel aspect of these restitution demands. By reinforcing the demand for a Jewish state, it dovetailed with Zionist ideology and politics. As World War II was winding down, the national claim for reparation emerged as a dual demand . . . This formulation constructed a fundamental connection between all Jews and Zionist ideology, thereby creating a modern national Jewish identity that had not existed previously . . . most Jews worldwide did not perceive themselves as having a national identity, nor were Jews recognized as a national entity by the world community. The Zionist movement after all had been supported by only a minority of the Jews. By killing off the majority of Jews in Europe, the extermination camps practically nullified such distinctions. For the Nazis, the Jews were a nation, a race, and an identity that had to be annihilated. This seeming affinity between the Zionist and Nazi definition of Jews as a nation/race has led, primarily since the eighties, to extensive and painful historical controversies. Was there affinity, conversion, or even collusion, at least in part, between Zionist and Nazi policies? In what way did such an embroilment contribute to the formation of Israel? But in the immediate period after the war even non-Zionist Jews were more inclined to accept the national definition, and to the rest of the world the Jewish people became precisely that: a people and a nation, not just a religion. The most significant consequence of these events was the international support for the creation of Israel (1948) as a Jewish homeland. Once established, the

Israeli government immediately assumed a leading role in representing Jewish interests globally.[18]

It is true that the reparations discussions of the 1990s that Torpey analyzes were separated by a period of 130 years or more from the abolition of slavery, whereas the Holocaust claims were settled within a shorter time span. But as Torpey acknowledges, the issue of slavery reparations goes back to 1865 at least. Robin Kelley and other historians have demonstrated that calls for some form of compensation for slavery continued to emerge in the period after slavery down to the present.[19] They did not necessarily use the legal language of reparations but were, instead, formulated as requests for land—forty acres and a mule—or ex-slave pensions.[20] None of these were supported by the US government. Instead, they were rejected, stymied, and ridiculed.

Torpey's periodization of reparations politics as a new phenomenon that is symptomatic of a postmodern decline of future-oriented ideologies is hard to maintain when one reviews the abundant evidence showing that proposals to compensate formally enslaved people were made in the nineteenth and twentieth centuries. It is also far from clear why asking for reparations for a crime that happened more than a hundred years ago is more retrospective than the nationalist political movements Torpey describes as future oriented. Many nationalist ideologies assert ancient origins as the basis of their authority and legitimacy. While reparations politics may not be as inclusive as socialist programs, most nationalist movements are highly exclusive as well. What is nationalism if not a form of identity politics? Political Zionism, an ideology that makes territorial claims based on events that happened millennia ago, and which can hardly be called inclusive and universalistic in its attitude toward Palestinians, is a case in point.

18 Elazar Barkan, *The Guilt of Nations: Restitution and Negotiating Historical Injustices* (New York: Norton, 2000), 5–6.

19 Robin D. G. Kelley, "'A Day of Reckoning': Dreams of Reparations," in Michael T. Martin and Marilyn Yaquinto, eds., *Redress for Historical Injustices in the United States: On Reparations for Slavery, Jim Crow, and Their Legacies* (Durham, NC: Duke University Press, 2007), 203–21.

20 Mary Frances Berry, *My Face Is Black Is True: Callie House and the Struggle for Ex-Slave Reparations* (New York: Vintage, 2006).

Torpey's book disregards the diversity of the political views that are held by reparations advocates and the complexity of their ideologies. To take just one example, which I already referred to in the previous chapter, an important group to have advocated reparations for slavery, the Republic of New Africa, presents such payments as part of a broader strategy that could easily be described as future oriented. Indeed, they propose to found a new and independent nation in the southern part of what is now the United States. For some reason, Torpey does not take this idea seriously. Of course, he would have every right to be doubtful about the progressive credentials of a project to found a new ethnonationalist state without regard to the wishes of the people who already live within its proposed borders. But being progressive and being future oriented are not necessarily the same thing.

Reparations for slavery are not exclusively a Black nationalist idea, however, and many advocates believe reparations should be part of a process of reconciliation within existing nation states. Since the publication of Torpey's book, the idea of reparations for slavery has become more widely accepted by figures in the mainstream media and politics in several countries, even if the policy remains unpopular among a great deal of people polled. As I explained, several politicians in the Democratic Party have now endorsed some form of reparations for slavery and used patriotic rhetoric to justify such measures. Repairing the legacies of slavery would, on this view, be another step along the way to fulfilling America's promise to be a truly inclusive democracy. Activists have sometimes presented reparations as a way to resolve the unfinished business of Reconstruction. The slogan "forty acres and a mule" reminds us that postwar commitments to address the economic consequences of centuries of slavery were never met. But the Reconstruction amendments to the Constitution were intended to make a transition possible. Section 2 of the Thirteenth Amendment of the US Constitution has been widely interpreted as authorizing the US Congress to legislate against "badges and incidents of slavery." Although there is no agreement about what precisely these terms mean, on a broad reading it could "encompass any public or private practice that 'perpetuates [racial] inferiority.'"[21] This could provide a

21 Jennifer Mason McAward, "Defining the Badges and Incidents of Slavery," *Journal of Constitutional Law* 14, no. 3 (2012).

constitutional basis for a form of transitional justice that has been too long delayed.

Others have argued that reparations must go beyond the narrow national level, and, instead, be reconceived as a global initiative. Probably the most important of the recent books on reparations is Olúfẹmi O. Táíwò's philosophical intervention on the topic, *Reconsidering Reparations*. The author presents a "constructive view" of reparations, understood as a question of distributive justice. He writes that "reparations are a worldmaking project . . . the relationship of persons to resources is not a static, one-time transaction. Resources flow to and away from people continuously."[22] His argument is based in the historical understanding that the modern world system has been set up to distribute advantages and disadvantages in a particular way, and that reparations proposals should aim to radically change the contours of "Global Racial Empire." Thinking on this broader scale is essential, because the climate change that the imperial system has produced will have adverse effects on the world population with a more severe impact on formerly colonized areas and historically marginalized groups.[23] Táíwò uses the metaphor of a water-management system to describe the structure of the world system, and states that "instead of water, advantages and disadvantages [drain] from one place to another."[24] Reparations should aim to change this distributive infrastructure. In other words, it must be a project of structural change, not a simple one-time transfer of money from one group to another.

The structure of racism

Reparations advocates have thus articulated a wide array of future-oriented goals ranging from symbolic redress to reconciliation to national self-determination. Across these different views however, there is a common aspiration to use such initiatives to procure funding that could be used to tackle the complex and deeply rooted problem of racism. That

22 Olúfẹmi O. Táíwò, *Reconsidering Reparations: Worldmaking in the Case of Climate Crisis* (Oxford: Oxford University Press, 2022), 20.

23 Ibid., 157.

24 Ibid., 20.

is to say, proposals for reparations for slavery and colonialism are not simply about compensation, they are usually presented as a means to rectify in some way the legacies of those systems; the most important manifestation of which is a form of racism which is so deeply ingrained in the contemporary world that it can be described as structural.

There has been a noticeable increase in the use of the adjective "structural," or "systemic," in public discussions about racism. The term is commonly used in the United States, but it has been taken up in other countries as well. It is intended to underline the fact that any solution to the problem of racism must involve a transformation of factors that are, at once, political, social, cultural, economic, and psychological in character. Thus defined, "structural racism" is a phenomenon with "material" and "symbolic" dimensions that affect all of society (and perhaps all societies).

Proposing to tackle something so complex and deeply ingrained in daily practices can hardly be called a narrow "identitarian" project. It is precisely because racism is understood as a structure—not as simply a problem of "mis-recognition," or of the attitudes of individuals and their perceptions of the identities—that reparations advocates insist that significant resources must be marshaled if the problem is ever to be resolved. If racism is structural, then overcoming it would be tantamount to a social-symbolic transformation on a grand scale. Surely, such a project could be described as "utopian."[25] In fact, the idea of surpassing or dismantling structural racism can be called utopian in a double sense: Since it is a call to produce a sea change in the general state of affairs, it is also vulnerable to the charge of being unrealistic. What, after all, would the destruction of structural racism and the establishment of a non-racist society or global order involve exactly? There is a notable lack of clearly articulated plans for the achievement of such a transformation beyond certain first steps, and there is certainly no consensus about what a non-racist society would look like. This ambiguity is typical of all political projects that have been called utopian. One need only think of the multiplicity of proposed paths to communism for

25 In this connection, Robin D. G. Kelley points out that so many of the critiques of identity politics in the 1990s ignored the broader "universalistic" goals those groups articulated. The Combahee River Collective's 1977 statement has been used to "demonstrate how narrow identity politics can get." But the statement actually calls for a universal socialist program. Robin D. G. Kelley, *Yo' Mama's Disfunktional!: Fighting the Culture Wars in Urban America* (Boston: Beacon Press, 1997), 111.

example. The passage to a world without racism would undoubtedly be a complex undertaking.

A practical antiracist politics must always pose the question of what combination of measures would most efficiently corrode racism. The answer would likely depend on the concrete circumstances of the particular society in which it is asked. One must consider the short- and long-term effects of any course of action. Sympathetic critics have, for instance, commonly argued that no matter how well-intentioned reparations policies may be, they run the risk of worsening the problem of racist resentment, if a large segment of the population views them as being punitive. But what alternatives are there and what risks do they entail? Would socialism resolve racism as a matter of course? Should, for example, the destruction of racism involve the abandonment of racial categories and identities altogether? Is that even possible? If so, is it desirable to wipe out the collective memories and identities of groups that have existed for generations? The answer to such questions obviously depends, in no small measure, on how racism itself is understood and defined.

The so-called color-blind approach to solving the problem of racism takes a clear position on these questions: If there is to be a solution to racism, then racial categories and identities must be abandoned and forgotten. Such proposals have been widely criticized for a number of reasons, and their sincerity has been questioned.[26] And yet for all its faults, the color-blind approach is at least a logically consistent answer to the question of how racism can be eradicated. If everyone were to magically lose their ability to distinguish skin colors, then the problem of racism might indeed disappear as a nameable phenomenon. But the color-blind approach is rooted in a simplistic conception that racism is

26 A key text on this is Eduardo Bonilla-Silva, *Racism Without Racists: Color-Blind Racism and the Persistence of Racial Inequality in the United States* (Lanham: Rowman & Littlefield, 2006). It has also been noted that color-blindism is usually invoked as a rhetorical strategy to dismiss concrete antiracist policies which are forced to name racism in order to combat it. Also see Kenan Van de Mieroop, "On the Advantages and Disadvantages of Black History Month for Life: The Creation of the Post-Racial Era," *History and Theory* (2016): 3–24. The French state's official embrace of this approach provides an empirical example of its obvious shortcomings in practice. In the Netherlands, too, Gloria Wekker notes that "dominant discourse stubbornly maintains that the Netherlands is and always has been color-blind and antiracist," even if this is empirically false as she shows. Gloria Wekker, *White Innocence: Paradoxes of Colonialism and Race* (Durham, NC: Duke University Press, 2016), 1.

primarily a problem of bigotry, and irrational hatred toward people who have particular physical traits. It construes racism in purely idealist terms.

The modifier "structural" is used to emphasize the fact that racism is deeply embedded in social relations, or that racism can function "without racists" as Eduardo Bonilla-Silva has put it. The color-blind solution is a fantasy precisely because the problem goes well beyond individual attitudes; rather, it has structural foundations. Racism is a social fact that no individual can simply wish away. But this deep-rootedness of racism does not mean that there is nothing at all that can be done about it. Like other social structures, racism is historical; it had a beginning, and thus, it can also be brought to an end.

The dominant framework for thinking about the question of racism in American scholarship takes a social-constructivist approach and highlights the fact that the numerous disparities between parts of the population have historical roots. Such disparities can easily be documented—and in the United States they are documented—by statistics that show large discrepancies in wealth and income, rates of incarceration, health outcomes, and numerous other measures. In the aggregate, all of these amount to a multifaceted, and deeply entrenched system of oppression that divides "racial" groups. Yet while social-constructivist accounts of structural racism are common both in public discourse and in scholarship, there is nevertheless no consensus about the precise, social-scientific definition of the concept.

Writing in the *New Left Review*, the sociologist Loïc Wacquant has criticized what he views as the casual use of the term "structural racism," claiming it is more of a political slogan than a precise category of analysis:

> Clumpy terms such as "structural racism" or "systemic racism," which, in the wake of social movements for racial justice have spread at blinding speed in the past few years—in part through the influence of think tanks and philanthropic foundations eager to rephrase old programmes in the new Racespeak of the moment—may work well as political mottos to mobilize people and to give them a personal sense of moral zeal and civic benevolence; they are nonetheless poor guides for dissecting, and thence overturning, the racial order.

He continues: "'Structural racism' posits that which needs to be discovered and demonstrated. It obfuscates the primacy of class disparity in criminal processing."[27] Wacquant's strong reaction to much of the well-meaning discourse on the "structural" elements of the phenomenon of racism is grounded in social-scientific as well as political concerns and animated by a desire to avoid the pitfalls of the "race vs. class" debate. Refining the conceptual tools of the sociology of "ethnoracial domination" is essential to dismantling racist practices in the real world.[28] Wacquant, who is from France but works in the United States, points out something that is obvious to anyone outside the English-speaking world—namely, that scholarship focusing on the American case has a central "Archimedean" position in scientific discourse on racism. Since one of his main concerns as a sociologist is to find categories of analysis that can be deployed to study racism in different contexts around the world, he believes it is imperative to decenter the United States. He does not elaborate on the reasons for the dominance of the American discussion on the topic, but one may assume that it is a reflection of the primacy of English-language scholarship in global academia in general. It may also have to do with the fact that antiracist movements in the United States have had more success in putting racism on the agenda of scientific research than has been the case in other countries. Meanwhile, as the European Network Against Racism points out, the United Kingdom is the only country in Europe that keeps statistics on disparities between "racial groups."[29] Such data—readily available in the US and the UK—facilitates the search for "systemic" or "structural" patterns of racism in a society. Where no such data exists, as is the case in France, for example, other methods must be used.[30] It is no surprise then, that when antiracist activists around the world look for a conceptual tool kit

27 Loïc Wacquant, "Resolving the Trouble with 'Race,'" *New Left Review* 133/134 (January–April 2022): 86–7.

28 Ibid., 80.

29 "Equality Data," ENAR, enar-eu.org.

30 Sometimes attitudes can be inferred from other data. On the topic of reparations, for instance, an article in *Le Figaro*, reported that an Ifop poll indicated that 63 percent of residents of French overseas departments are in favor of reparations "whether moral or financial." "Le cran veut poursuivre la caisse des dépôts pour avoir 'profité de L'esclavage,'" *Le Figaro*, May 10, 2013, lefigaro.fr. Pap Ndiaye discusses the question of how research can proceed under these conditions in *La Condition Noire: Essai sur une minorité française* (Paris: Calman-Levy, 2008).

to analyze the racism that afflicts their own societies, they draw inspiration from the scholarship and activism that has examined these issues in the United States. Representations of racism and antiracism in American popular culture have spread around the world. In my opinion, this dynamic has produced much good and has been important in opening up a space for the discussion of racism in the public discourse of many countries. Even so, one can only conclude that Wacquant's concerns about the extent to which scholarship on the American case is transferable to other contexts are justified. The term "structural racism," for example, is audible in European contexts, but it seems likely that the "structural" nature of racism in many countries may differ significantly. Wacquant reminds us of the peculiarity of "the American definition of race as civic felony and of blackness as public dishonour transmitted through strict hypodescent are historical outliers. No other ethnic group in the United States is bounded on that basis and no other society on the planet defines blackness thus."[31]

If "structural racism" is too loose a term, then what does Wacquant propose as an alternative? He introduces some key ideas that should inform a robust theory of the dynamics of ethnoracial domination across disparate societies, adding the disclaimer that what he is proposing is more of a starting point than a finished and closed conceptual framework. Three elements of his proposal are particularly compelling. They are, first of all, a denial of the idea that "race" is fundamentally different from "ethnicity." Even self-proclaimed social constructivists frequently fall for the illusion that "race" can be ontologically distinguished from ethnicity. This is mistaken because racism is precisely the insistence that ethnic differences are rooted in nature or biology and are not open to change.

Wacquant's second contribution is to elaborate some of the components of ethnoracial domination that go beyond the vague term "structural racism" and point to more specific mechanisms that might well be present in multiple societies around the world, not only in the United States. He speaks of five aspects or "elementary forms of racial domination." This "pentad" includes categorization, discrimination, segregation, ghettoization, and violence. These forms do not always appear with the same intensity in every instance. Wacquant notes how

31 Wacquant, "Resolving the Trouble with 'Race,'" 71.

they can interact and develop over time, and that one group—for example, "African Americans in the United States"—has faced "different profiles of *ethnoracial domination across time* and space."[32] To show the applicability of his categories of analysis beyond the dominant American case, he briefly discusses how the Roma in Europe also face these five elements of domination, and how they employ strategies to evade and resist them.

The third important contribution he makes, builds on the first point that "race is a subtype of ethnicity," not something separate.[33] "Race" is a product of the "racialization" of ethnicity. He presents a model for plotting different forms of ethnoracial domination along an ideal-typical scale of racialization. On the lefthand side of the horizontal axis, ethnicity is understood to be "thin" and "malleable." It is broadly recognized as being an element of culture, and the product of a historical development that is, to some degree, "arbitrary," open to change and often self-chosen (that is to say, that individuals choose to identify themselves as a belonging to a particular *ethnos*).[34] At this end of the scale there is a high "social estimation of honour."[35] On the opposite end, social estimation of honor is low: "'Thick' ethnicity denies its own historicity (which thus becomes covert) and claims to be rooted in the necessity of nature and biology (or its logical analogue, culture understood as hard-wired and virtually unchanging), materialized in its most extreme form by caste and caste-like arrangements."[36] Racialization then, is the fixing and "naturalization" of ethnic differences, a denial of historicity and a concomitant public dishonoring of particular groups.

This way of visualizing the dynamic of racialization is, I think, very useful because it is flexible enough to take account of different geographical and historical contexts. It also provides an interesting way to think about the hierarchies of discrimination that are visible in most societies, whereby some groups face more severe ethnoracial domination than others. Moreover, these categories could potentially be used in a historical account of the development and change in the mechanisms that

32 Ibid., 80 (emphasis in original).
33 Ibid., 85.
34 Ibid., 76.
35 Here Wacquant uses a concept of honor taken from Max Weber.
36 Ibid., 76–7.

racialize one particular group. In order to develop his categories of analysis, Wacquant is necessarily obliged to present them synchronically, as though frozen at one moment in time. Absent from his account is any elaboration of how his pentad of ethnoracial domination and his scale of racialization might be used for diachronic analyses. But it would only take a little imagination to use his categories for a historical study of the development of racialization over time. In other words, we can use these categories to track the deepening racialization of particular groups. This would be a movement down the scale of racialization.

Conversely, Wacquant's scheme also provides a way to ponder the main question that has been posed in this chapter—namely, what would the process of de-racialization involve? This question can now be understood in a new way: What combination of measures would facilitate a movement up the scale of racialization, back toward malleable and thin ethnicity? In other words, what project or projects could be designed that would effectively de-racialize ethnic groups by dismantling caste-like arrangements, and thinning out "thick" and naturalized categorizations of humans? Presented in this way, antiracism seems like an achievable project that can be broken down into concrete steps instead of as a final "racial reckoning" or moment of justice. Though the danger of slipping back down into dynamics of racialization would always remain.

Using his framework, it immediately becomes clear why any movement on the scale of racialization—whether upward or downward—must involve a combination of "material" and "symbolic" factors. Perhaps we can parse these analytically, but in the social world, they are intertwined. Wacquant does not explain the ways in which his five elementary forms interact and reinforce one another. It seems, however, that there is a reciprocal relationship between the different elements that produces a vicious circle: discrimination, segregation, ghettoization, and violence are all motivated, inspired, and justified by categorization. Categorization is here defined as "assignation to a hierarchical and naturalizing classification system encompassing prejudice, bias and stigma."[37] But, surely, such categorizations, in turn, are considered persuasive by some social actors because of the ways in which they appear to correspond to the observed social situation and because they

37 Ibid., 80.

offer a way to explain, describe, and justify it. Recognizing and even embracing—or strategically using—ethnoracial categorizations can also be part of acts of resistance and self-defense. Paul Gilroy reminds us that one of the reasons that it is hard to convince people to abandon problematic category of "race" is not only that so many "beneficiaries of racial hierarchy do not want to give up their privileges" but also that

> people who have been subordinated by race-thinking and its distinctive social structures (not all of which come tidily color-coded) have for centuries employed the concepts and categories of their rulers, owners and persecutors to resist the destiny that "race" has allocated to them and to dissent from the lowly value it placed upon their lives.[38]

The intertwining of the symbolic and material dimensions of racism requires further elaboration, in my opinion. Wacquant suggests that racial categorizations are ahistorical, in the sense that they are naturalizing and deny the historical contingency of ethnic differences. But he forgets to mention that racial categorizations are often presented precisely as theories of historical development. This is one way in which the idea of "race" functions as an instrument of temporality. Sometimes, these are explicitly spelled out (as in social Darwinist accounts or the Hamitic hypothesis), and other times, they remain inchoate (as in the case of those who claim that there are significant IQ differences between "races" and then suggest—by implication rather than formal argument—that observed inequalities across groups are the product of genetic rather than environmental factors). "Racial" categorizations serve to explain visible social inequality and the conditions that go along with it. Racism provides a rudimentary social scientific theory that purports to account for the poverty and "underdevelopment" of the African continent and racialized people in the diaspora. It provides a rationale for anti-migration policies and exploitative neocolonial relations of economic exploitation dressed up as "development." And these ideas in turn motivate and inform new acts of discrimination, segregation, ghettoization, and violence. This dynamic illustrates well

38 Paul Gilroy, *Against Race: Imagining Political Culture Beyond the Color Line* (Cambridge, MA: Belknap Press, 2000), 12.

Pierre Bourdieu's critique of the distinction between objectivist and subjectivist positions in social science. A student of Bourdieu, Wacquant cites his teacher's argument that subjective perceptions form part of objective "social reality," and conversely, that said reality is "an object of perception."[39] In other words, as Paul Gilroy explains "'race' [is] an active, dynamic idea or principle that assists in the constitution of social reality."[40]

Epidermalization: Stuart Hall and the semiotics of "race"

Calling racism an object of perception is an understatement of course. Visual spectacle is one of the most pronounced features of this form of social domination. The whole system of categorization is culturally encoded in the physical traits of individuals. In this way, the ideology of racism becomes a visible part of the observed social world as "embodied alterity, hierarchy and temporality."[41] Stuart Hall's analysis of the imaginary, symbolic, and fetishistic dimensions of racism foreground issues that are overlooked in Wacquant's account. Hall cites Fanon: "I am a slave, not of an idea that others have of me, but of my own appearance, I am fixed by it." Fanon remarks here on the fact that the whole history of slavery is carried as the connotative content of his own outward appearance in the eyes of his racist society; it is epidermalized. Hall detects the same insight in Du Bois's metaphor of the "badge": "Because color, though of little meaning in itself, is really important, Du Bois argues, 'as a *badge* for the social heritage of slavery, the dissemination and the insult of that experience.'" Hall's insight that "race works like a language" has

39 Bourdieu, quoted in ibid., 74. Further down Wacquant explains: "Racial phenomenology is integral to racial reality in a way that is not true of other bases of stratification—that is: classes exist, if potentially, in the absence of class consciousness; not so ethnoracial groups in the absence of ethnically inflected cognition (if only by the dominant). Put differently, *race is a pure modality of symbolic violence*, the bending of social reality to fit a mental map of reality; or, to put it more tersely still, a limiting case of the *realization of categories*, the conundrum at the heart of Bourdieu's sociology."

40 Here he is commenting on Eric Voegelin's explanation that racism's "function is not to describe social reality but to assist in its constitution." Voegelin cited in Gilroy, *Against Race*, 57–8.

41 Ibid., 58.

profound implications: The semiotic approach underlines the way in which bodily traits are historically linked to a range of signifieds. In the language of racism, skin color connotes; racialized bodies are read like texts.[42] There is no need to list here the wide range of stereotypes and signifieds that skin color can call up in the minds of those who inhabit societies structured along ethnoracial lines. When skin is so encoded, it becomes a temporal tool and reflective instrument: It transmits traditions of distinction in what Ricoeur described as a language-like manner.

If we are to give this semiotic dynamic a place in Wacquant's schema, we should locate it under what he calls "categorization." But it seems more accurate to say that the whole system of ethnoracial categorization is one of the connotations carried by the racialized body. In other words, skin color, like a mnemonic device, can evoke a whole system of categorization. Categorizations which, as I said earlier, not only function as taxonomies of contemporary individuals but sometimes amount to an explanation and justification for the historical development and continued existence of the ethnoracial domination. Is not this precisely the point that is illustrated by Roland Barthes's famous semiotic analysis of the cover of *Paris Match*? A simple photograph of a racialized body can covey an entire mythology to someone waiting to get his haircut at the barber shop. His well-known essay explains how the cover of the glossy magazine which shows a "young Negro in a French uniform . . . saluting, with his eyes uplifted, probably fixed on a fold of the tricolour" actually conveys a deeper ideological point "that France is a great Empire, that all her sons, without any colour discrimination, faithfully serve under her flag, and that there is no better answer to the detractors of an alleged colonialism than the zeal shown by this Negro in serving his so-called oppressors."[43]

The analysis reveals that the skin color of the boy in question has been loaded with a symbolism that goes beyond stereotype. Skin color interacts with other signs on the cover of the magazine to call up an entire mythology of historical progress and conceptions of civilization and barbarity.

42 Stuart Hall, "Race, the Floating Signifier [1997]," in *Writings on Race and Difference*, ed. Paul Gilroy and Ruth Wilson Gilmore (Durham, NC: Duke University Press, 2021), 359–73 (my emphasis). Transcript available at Media Education Foundation, mediaed.org.

43 Roland Barthes, *Mythologies*, trans. Annette Lavers (New York: Noonday Press, 1972), 115.

Hall advances the semiotic analysis of racism much further. His 1997 lecture on the subject focuses on the implications of the fact that signs are slippery and can never be fully grounded:

> Signifiers refer to the systems and concepts of the classification of a culture, to its practices for making meaning. And those things gain their meaning, not because of what they contain in their essence, but in the shifting relations of difference, which they establish with other concepts and ideas in a signifying field. Their meaning, because it is relational, and not essential, can never be finally fixed, but is subject to the constant process of redefinition and appropriation: to the losing of old meanings, and appropriation and collection and contracting of new ones, to the endless process of being constantly resignified, made to mean something different in different cultures, in different historical formations at different moments of time.
>
> The meaning of a signifier can never be finally or transhistorically fixed. That is, it is always, or there is always, a certain sliding of meaning, always a margin not yet encapsulated in language and meaning, always something about race left unsaid.[44]

The relationship between signifiers and signifieds in racist symbolic systems is an arbitrary one, in the sense that Ferdinand de Saussure used that term when he discussed the nature of the sign. And yet, as analysts of systems of ethnoracial domination, we must explain the fact that "racial" signifiers *are fixed* by speakers of the language of "race," if not transhistorically, then for very long periods of time. After all, the stereotypes and cultural connotations that were encoded in skin color decades or centuries ago continue to be recognized today. This characteristic of racism is precisely why it was, and is, deployed. It has always been used as a temporal instrument to reproduce relations of domination and distinction over time. Skin color marked the division between enslaved labor (which lasted for life and was hereditary) and indentured servitude (which lasted for a limited time) or waged labor.

If the relationship between the signifier and signified is not fixed by nature, then how can we account for the incredible longevity of

44 Hall, "Race, the Floating Signifier."

racialized signs? The answer to that question is not fully spelled out by Hall in that specific lecture, but can be deduced: "Racial" signs become fixed through daily reinforcement and practices of racism which constitute the visible "*parole*" that is informed, ordered, and constrained by the virtual but objective "*langue*" of ethnoracial domination—a domination that is composed of the pentad of elementary forms which Wacquant describes. "Categorization" is not a purely theoretical or reflective exercise that remains in the realm of ideas; it contributes to the habitus of actors in a radicalized field.

The symbolic aspects of systems of ethnoracial domination are thus firmly linked to material conditions, or to what Bourdieu calls an "economy of symbolic exchanges" in *Language and Symbolic Power*.[45] The "intellectualist" approach to language has presented it primarily as an "object of intellection" rather than an instrument of action and power.[46] Against this paradigm, Bourdieu insists that language use operates like a market. The market not only contributes to the value of the communication but also plays a role in determining its very meaning.[47] Language is constrained and must be used strategically, depending on one's place in a particular field. Not all users of a language can claim to have the same illocutionary power. The observation seems applicable to racism as well. If racism is a language understood by all groups in a racialized society, this does not imply that each individual can use it to the same effect. Racist practices—among those, Wacquant's five elementary forms—have the effect of constraining and fixing this semantic slippage and creating the material conditions that push the dynamic of racialization to the righthand side of his scale.

Transforming traditions: Dismantling ethnoracial domination

Antiracist political projects should aim to move back up to the left of the scale. But how? To reiterate a question posed earlier: What would the dismantling and destruction of this symbolic system require? If we take

45 Pierre Bourdieu, *Langage et pouvoir symbolique* (Paris: Points, 2014), 60.

46 Ibid., 59.

47 Ibid., 61. According to Bourdieu: "Grammar defines meaning only partially, and the complete determination of the meaning of discourse takes place in relation to a market." Ibid., 60 (my translation).

the foregoing analysis seriously, then we must conclude that the distinction sometimes drawn by activists and scholars between "symbolic" and "material" aspects is perhaps unhelpful because these are inevitably intertwined.

To be sure, the symbolic aspect is of central importance. Antiracist projects should aim to evacuate the semantic content from "racial" characteristics that have been transformed into signifiers. We can—as Ricoeur would say—take a stance on this tradition. But it is naive to believe that the sediments of semantic content that have been encoded in a set of bodily traits over generations can easily be erased or forgotten overnight, and without any alteration to the conditions that give this symbolic system its force. "Raciology has saturated the discourses in which it circulates. It cannot be readily re-signified."[48]

Returning then to the issue of reparations, it should be clear why purely symbolic approaches to solving the issue of racism will not work. Consider that the official apologies and expressions made by governments for the crimes of slavery and colonialism have done little to reverse or overcome the problem of racism, even if they may have been meaningful for many people. In Hollywood films and television programming, one finds abundant attempts to achieve reconciliation through fiction.[49] Racist stereotypical depictions or descriptions of certain (but certainly not all) groups have been gradually weeded out of a great deal of media production in the English-speaking world. Racist pseudoscientific discourse and social Darwinist accounts have been completely debunked and discredited in academia in these same countries. While all of these are positive developments, they have evidently not been sufficient.

What historical process would then be sufficient to empty the semantic content from racist signs? Few precedents exist. But Reinhart Koselleck has shown that the historical development of concepts of time reflects complex social transitions. For instance, the radical changes that occurred during the period he calls saddle time effected a rupture so intense that the old phrase *historia magistra vitae* no longer appeared to make sense. It persisted as a sort of husk emptied of its content—a relic

48 Gilroy, *Against Race*, 12.

49 A great analysis of this is offered in Mark Golub, "History Died for Our Sins: Guilt and Responsibility in Hollywood Redemption Histories," *Journal of American Culture* 21 (1998): 23–45.

of a previous system.[50] Crucially, in his argument, there was a break between the lived experiences of historical time and of temporality which rendered the topos irrelevant. To effect this semantic shift and disrupt an idea that had been considered persuasive since antiquity, it took nothing less than a period of massive upheaval and revolutionary change, *Sattelzeit*, and it coincided with the coming to dominance of a new mode of production.

Is it reasonable to assume that current systems of ethnoracial domination can be overturned without something resembling a new *Sattelzeit*?[51] Any project to bring about progress on this scale could hardly be described as narrow and identitarian. On the other hand, one could well ask why such a project should be placed under the heading "reparations." While it is possible to conceive of reparations as an occasion for radical systemic change, one might argue that it would be easier to present the same ambitions in a different political vocabulary. The term "reparations" is overburdened. My own view is that reparations should be understood as a means to an end rather than as an end in itself. It is unlikely that a "racial reckoning" or moment of justice, during which the problem of racism and the legacies of slavery are historically transcended, will ever arrive. An achievable goal might be to focus on reorganizing relations of ownership, production, and distribution in contemporary societies, and on dismantling the pentad of domination. Doing so could undermine the "economy of symbolic exchanges" that gives racism its currency. Reparations might in certain cases be deployed as a useful tool along the way to pursuing such a reorganization, but such reparations need not be conflated with the reorganization itself.

50 Reinhart Koselleck, "Historia Magistra Vitae: The Dissolution of the Topos into the Perspective of a Modernized Historical Process," in *Futures Past*, trans. Keith Tribe (New York: Columbia University Press, 2004), 27–43.

51 In any case, we can say for certain that even the period of great upheaval that was *Sattelzeit* was not sufficient to undermine European racialism. Cedric Robinson notes that instead "the shift in eighteenth-century and nineteenth-century Western thought from a basis of a religious and philosophical epistemology to that of modern science had made little difference. In point of fact, it had merely served to extend the terms and rationales for the fantasy of racial inferiority (for the Jews, Irish, Slavs, and Asians as well as for Blacks). Western scientific thought simply took its place as the latest formal grammar for the expression of a racial metaphysics." Cedric Robinson, *Black Marxism: The Making of the Black Radical Tradition* (Chapel Hill: University of North Carolina Press, 2000), 76.

6

A New Temporality?

The tradition of all dead generations weighs like a nightmare on the brains of the living.
—Karl Marx, *The Eighteenth Brumaire of Louis Bonaparte*

Racism's changing same does triple duty: claims of natural *or* cultural *incommensurabilites secure conditions for reproducing* economic *inequalities, which then validate theories of extra-economic hierarchical difference.*
—Ruth Wilson Gilmore, *Abolition Geography*

We will make a clean slate of the past
Enslaved masses, rise up, rise up!
—Eugène Pottier and Pierre De Geyter, *L'internationale*, 1871

The reproduction of the relations of production and ethnoracial domination

Now that the death knell of *woke* has been vigorously sounded by the triumphant right and parts of the left, some may wonder if it announces the end of reparations talk. The former present reparations for slavery and colonialism as a synecdoche for the type of politics that has emasculated the West. The latter, meanwhile, have placed the blame for recent defeats on identity politics and, in the name of pragmatism, called for a more class-focused approach. In this climate, it is difficult to imagine that lawsuits for reparations will succeed, and one may indeed wonder whether tabling proposals in legislatures makes strategic sense.

Others will no doubt see what we are currently witnessing as the eternal return of racist reaction. Calls for reparations have always been treated with skepticism and hostility, and there is no reason to believe they will now be silenced. Interstate claims will remain an important diplomatic issue as indebted countries continue to confront their creditors in the metropoles of global capitalism. Indeed, a number of governments across the West and the Middle East are likely to face new reparations demands for their role in the genocide of the Palestinians. And, perhaps most importantly, even if the left were to abandon reparations talk and forgo the legalistic language of crime, debt, restitution, and repair, the fundamental question at the heart of these proposals will remain. The crux of the matter is, of course, the following question: How can we dismantle a mode of production and ethnoracial domination that has reproduced itself for so many generations and continues to manifest in new forms? Any movement that wishes to call itself emancipatory must attempt to present solutions to this problem.

Throughout this book, I have laid out the ways in which reparations proposals have been construed as exhibiting a pathological relationship to time—either as a mode of retrospective politics which reflects a general discombobulation brought about by the rapid pace of change in postmodernity, or as a form of collective resentment—and I have sought to bring to light the historical theories and assumptions about temporality that form the basis for that appraisal. The most recurrent intellectual, political, moral, and legal arguments against reparations for slavery and colonialism focus on what is deemed to be the perverse temporal logic which these calls for redress appear to entail. When activists demand reparations, they are told not to dwell on the past and are reminded that the statute of limitations has passed. They are chided for suggesting that guilt, debt, or responsibility can be transmitted across generations by the very same people who call for a return to tradition and national identity. They are informed that it is impossible to put a price on past suffering, even though these principles have been adhered to in other cases. They are admonished for insisting on talking about "race" and told it is *they* who are guilty of perpetuating racism by clinging to the past instead of believing, against all evidence, that racism will disappear if we simply choose to forget it. All these arguments are informed by a sentiment that events which happened long ago are of minimal relevance now.

Reparations talk turns this reasoning around. It begins from the premise that the exploitation and domination of multitudes of racialized people around the world today is impossible to understand, let alone ameliorate, without referring to the legacies of slavery and colonialism. The remarkable longevity and stubbornness of the mode of production and ethnoracial domination that slavery and colonialism played a significant role in producing, expanding, and developing is precisely the problem that needs to be addressed. What explains its continued reproduction from one generation to the next? What measures can be taken to break its vicious cycle?

The first question has been investigated, most thoroughly, by Cedric Robinson, who suggested that the cycle we are caught up in today has roots that go back to the "very beginnings of European civilization."[1] He presents a history of "racialism" across four broad epochs or distinct moments, beginning with a "formative period" in the Middle Ages, passing through a phase of reaction to "Islamic domination" of the Mediterranean, followed by a reformulation during the "merchant capitalist" expansion into the New World, culminating in "the dialectic of colonialism, plantocratic slavery, and resistance from the sixteenth century forward, and the formations of industrial labor and labor reserves" and down to the present day.[2] The breadth of examples and time periods he draws upon serve to demonstrate that the imbrication of feudal and capitalist modes of production—both of which divide labor and differentiate producers and appropriators of surplus value—with practices and ideologies of racialism is not incidental but intrinsic. "The tendency of European civilization through capitalism was thus not to homogenize but to differentiate—to exaggerate regional, subcultural, and dialectical

1 Cedric Robinson, *Black Marxism: The Making of the Black Radical Tradition* (Chapel Hill: University of North Carolina Press, 2000), 67.

2 Ibid.

differences into 'racial' ones."[3] A mode of production predicated on expansion and differentiation leads, almost by necessity, to the emergence of ever new forms of ethnoracial domination. This is why "racial capitalism" is to be understood as a composite: "The development, organization, and expansion of capitalist society pursued essentially racial directions, so too did social ideology. As a material force, then, it could be expected that racialism would inevitably permeate the social structures emergent from capitalism."[4]

If Robinson is right, it becomes obvious that breaking this cycle is hardly a narrow and identitarian program but would, in fact, constitute a task of epochal significance. It also becomes clear why this task cannot be fully achieved within a capitalist framework. That is why so many writers and activists have criticized liberal antiracist policies as inadequate, and in some cases, perhaps counterproductive.[5] At the same time, while it is true that an approach based on an analysis rooted in understandings of class is essential, merely pointing this out is not sufficient. After all, even a class-based politics must still contend with the problem of what Henri Lefebvre called the survival of capitalism. Understanding why capitalism, in spite of its contradictions, continually reproduces itself, requires one to explain not only the reproduction of the means of production, but also of the relations of production.[6] That reproduction is ensured not only by ideological and repressive apparatuses—which are becoming increasingly sophisticated and powerful every day—but also by the distributions of space in which everyday life unfolds. "Space as a whole," Lefebvre notes, is where this reproduction is "located."[7] But this insight would be incomplete without adding, following Ruth Wilson Gilmore, that "race and space are mutually constituted."[8] Gilmore writes that "any map of modernity's fundamental features—growth, industrialization, articulation, urbanization, and inequality—as measured by wealth

3 Ibid., 26.

4 Ibid., 2.

5 See especially Arun Kundnani, *What Is Antiracism and Why It Means Anticapitalism* (London: Verso, 2023).

6 Henri Lefebvre, *The Survival of Capitalism: Reproduction of the Relations of Production*, trans. Frank Bryant (New York: St. Martin's Press, 1973), 9.

7 Ibid., 84.

8 Ruth Wilson Gilmore, *Abolition Geography: Essays Towards Liberation* (London: Verso, 2022), 120, ebook.

will also map historical-geographical racisms."[9] Racisms are historical-geographical because if power "is everywhere in space" it is also located in time.[10]

The designation, management, and distribution of time are likewise indispensable practices for any order that wishes to reproduce itself. Temporal tools and techniques of time management play a fundamental role in the reproduction of relations of production and domination. Power is always diachronic. But temporality, constructed to serve specific ends, can be contested by those who seek to promote different ones. The French revolutionaries were right to lay their finger on this problem. Emancipatory projects today must also develop strategies to overturn the temporalities that preserve capitalist accumulation and ethnoracial domination.

Lefebvre also observed that "power does not have a completely sure grip on any of its instruments. After all, there is nothing which says that the army, the police, the pigs, the *Tontons-macoutes* etc. cannot strike, revolt, want power in their turn or betray their master."[11] One of the reasons that reparations talk has sparked such ire is that those who have articulated these demands have appropriated existing temporal tools for their own ends. They have picked up instruments of domination and turned them on the powerful. Transgressions of this type cannot be tolerated.

Going against the grain of much of the commentary on the topic, I have attempted to make the case in this book that calls for reparations for slavery and colonialism are not, in fact, an extraordinary departure from the temporality of normal politics. Activists have actually drawn on existing and well-established moral and political ideas, so that the temporal logic implicit in their arguments for redress is hardly unique. Movements for reparation have deployed temporal instruments that are already commonly in use in the West, not invented new ones. Such movements are therefore not so much symptomatic of a new temporality as they are an example of a political conflict within the existing temporal framework of the societies in which these calls have been articulated. This conflict within the

9 Ibid., 121.

10 Lefebvre, *The Survival of Capitalism*, 86.

11 Ibid., 86.

frameworks of existing temporalities reveals a great deal about the temporal tools that organize the contemporary world and maintain relations of domination. To be sure, critics are entitled to find fault with the temporality that informs reparations claims. Nevertheless, they ought to understand that the principles of time management to which activists appeal are not only commonly used now but have been for centuries. Indeed, the idea of reparations is far older than the recent debates.[12]

I began by discussing the redundant demand—so often voiced in response to reparations claims—that politics should focus on the needs of the present. All politics do so, and those asking for reparations proceed with the conviction that they are addressing contemporary problems. The more difficult matter is to determine what those needs are and who is entitled to articulate them in the name of society in general. This is an issue of narrative representation in a double sense: It involves the problem of the representation of reality on the one hand and of political representation on the other. The second chapter examined the idea of the present in the history of philosophical reflection on time. Statements about the historical moment in which we are currently living involve the selection of chronologically disparate data and their emplotment into a narrative historical present. This practice is ideological, and defining the present moment is a key part of the political contest. Paul Ricoeur had underlined the political import of historical presents in *Time and Narrative.* But, as I have shown, the implicit subject of his hermeneutics of historical consciousness is a citizen of a modern nation-state. This problematic assumption places a limitation on his analysis of the politics of time and consequently avoids dealing with some important questions. For instance, there is the question of who narrates historical time in the name of society. When do such narratives interpellate historical subjects? How should his categories apply to the masses of people who do not fit easily into existing ethno-national categorizations? How might these categories function in the life of an enslaved person

12 Already in the twelfth century, a bishop demanded reparations from the Danes for the destruction of church property and the enslavement of Frenchmen at the hands of the Vikings. See Frederik Pedersen, "Payment for Past Crimes: 12th Century French Cleric Who Called on Denmark to Pay for Viking Raids," *Conversation*, August 17, 2022, theconversation.com.

upon whom, as Orlando Patterson showed, natal alienation and social death have been imposed? These questions are of central concern to activists who demand that reparations involve symbolic components such as historical education and apologies.

Of course, what is at stake in the current reparations debates is not the fate of the enslaved but of their successors. This point is frequently underlined by critics who also remark upon the outlandishness of asserting that guilt and responsibility might be inherited. Indeed, many supporters of reparations are also critical of the idea of hereditary guilt and debt. In an effort to circumvent such objections, a number of philosophers have set themselves the task of developing new normative theories of intergenerational justice that could accommodate reparations claims. To be sure, many of these theories are persuasive. But, as I argued in the third chapter, we should remember that advocates are not attempting to lay out new principles of heredity and transmission of responsibility. They are deliberately drawing on ideas that go back centuries or millennia and are well established as part of the conceptual register of the so-called modern West and Middle East. That tradition—like all traditions—has been marked by inconsistency and contradiction. Debates on the nature of heredity have taken on many forms over the years: from ancient Greek notions of "ancestral fault" and Christian ideas of original sin and the Hamitic curse, to modern ideas of transmission via national belonging and capitalist money. It is this tradition that Ta-Nehisi Coates calls upon when he cites the Hebrew Bible and John Locke in the epigraphs of his widely discussed article on reparations. At the same time, when the CARICOM and African countries request that European countries repay their debts for slavery and colonialism, they do so in part as a response to the claims upon their own sovereign debt made by creditors in the financial centers of the modern world. In the Abuja Declaration, the World Conference Against Racism, and in CARICOM's reparations plan, debt cancellation has been a central demand. These debt-encumbered countries are posing the question: Who really owes what to whom?

Whether one likes it or not, the main bodies that adjudicate conflicts within states and between them recognize the idiom of national responsibility and capitalist money. Settlements for the most heinous crimes are often made in money. It may indeed be morally repugnant to put a price on suffering, but as I explained in the fourth chapter of this book, the function of general-purpose money is to put a price on anything. Those who demand financial redress are, again, making use of an existing mechanism—money—not inventing it. Of course, it may reasonably be objected that such an extreme case pushes money's equative capacities to their limits—I share these widespread ethical concerns. At the same time, however, the attempts that have already been made to quantify the impact of historical slavery on the world today are fascinating for what they reveal about how money functions as an instrument of temporality. Money can reach across time and compare different epochs. As such, it underpins historical narratives—still prominent within economic discourse—of linear development. It homogenizes historical time.

Present-value calculations have been used by those who have attempted to price reparations claims. These methods of accounting are widely understood and regularly used; it is therefore logical for reparations advocates to reach for them. On the other hand, we would do well to remember that they are rooted in a fetishistic understanding of money. If, instead, one were to conceive of reparations calculations as an accounting in terms of what Marx called value, one would come to a different picture of the issues involved, even if it would suffer from the same ethical problems as conventional ones. Such an intellectual exercise would have implications that go beyond the case of reparations for slavery and reveal the history of capitalism itself in a new light. For one thing, it can immediately highlight the mutual intertwining of multiple different forms of labor exploitation. The interconnections are revealed by Marx's conception of money, which, under capitalism, functions as a temporal tool by rendering the concrete labor times of individuals commensurate as elements of a homogenous, socially necessary labor time. The money wealth of the contemporary world is dependent on past, current, and future labor. Historical economic development, seen from this perspective, is not so much linear as it is layered. Capital today, as Marx notes, is dead labor that must be re-valorized again and again. Breaking this cycle would require abandoning money in its current form.

Some have sought to present reparations as a broad project of social transformation that might include, or contribute to, a transition away from capitalism. For others, reparations fit within a liberal capitalist and nationalist framework. But despite the differences, most advocates point to the necessity of confronting racism head on. They tend to view racism as a structure that is not fully explained by economic analysis. In the fifth chapter of this book, I discussed Loïc Wacquant's suggestion that the structural nature of racism needs a more robust social-scientific explanation, and noted that it is incomplete if it does take into account the semiotic dimensions of the phenomenon that have been outlined most clearly by Stuart Hall. Moreover, the analysis of enthoracial domination must be extended diachronically. I argued that racism is a temporal instrument that works to reproduce relations of ethnoracial domination, and the regimes of accumulation which they facilitate. It also serves to epidermalize—to use a Fanonian term—an entire philosophy of history. These characteristics have ensured that racism is perpetuated over time and handed down from generation to generation. That is exactly the point of racism.

How can societies break with long traditions of racism? Both liberal and nationalist varieties of reparations politics present responses to this question. Liberal versions of a "racial reckoning" propose to sever the connection between inequality and "race" by ensuring that the money wealth held by each group in society is proportional to their share of the population. This wealth transfer is to be accompanied by a symbolic dimension that would consist in some form of atonement or solemn reflection on the history of racism. On the other hand, national separatist versions of reparations intend to preserve so-called racial identities and to establish new states for "African descendants" in which they will be honored and allowed to thrive.

If actually carried out, both of these projects may well succeed in ameliorating the lives of many people. But it is not at all certain that they will decisively contain the dynamic of ethnoracial domination in general. They may only displace it onto other groups. In any case, I cannot see how the first proposal could overcome what Cedric Robinson and others have described as racial capitalism or the tendency to racialize populations. Nationalist proposals might do better in this regard, on the condition that they are linked to the noncapitalist economic forms that so many activists have advocated. But every nationalist project in history has been plagued by chauvinistic tendencies, and there is no obvious reason why this case would be exceptional.

The question of how to bring about a moment of historical justice or racial reckoning is more theological than practical. Or, rather, the practicality of such calls lies in the way in which they deploy prophetic motifs to mobilize and motivate people in societies rooted in the traditions of the Abrahamic religions to struggle for an idea of justice. The tendency to conceive of reparations as a sort of utopian horizon and standpoint from which to criticize existing society is still more evidence that this form of politics draws from a deep cultural reservoir of temporal tools and historical ideas.

So far, then, reparations proposals have mostly pursued the politics of time within the boundaries of existing temporalities by drawing on recognized temporal tools. But a radical transition away from the current mode of production and ethnoracial domination might be achievable only if we break with the dominant modes of temporality that underpin these systems. But it is not very fair to dismiss reparations proposals on the grounds that they fall short of the utopian goal of overcoming ethnoracial domination if one cannot present a serious alternative strategy. After all, what would a rupture of this kind actually entail? I do not have all the answers to this question, to be sure. But I am convinced that it would demand a restructuring of the link between money, time, and value, and keep in mind Marx's statement in the *Grundrisse* that all economics ultimately comes down to an economy of time. It would have as its goal the construction of a society in which time management, at the levels of lived and historical time, would be understood, in part, as a collective project. The contours and needs of the present would continue to be the subject of perpetual democratic debate. It would also involve the development of new mechanisms for organizing the collectivity of free persons diachronically across generations. Problems of inheritance and intergenerational transmission would, of course, still have to be dealt with but new principles could be developed beyond the paradigms of money, property, and nation. Building such a mode of social organization on the foundations of a society that has been so thoroughly shaped by the legacies of slavery and colonialism is not a straightforward task. The racism that has been bequeathed to us will continue to contribute to the reproduction of relations of production and domination into the future unless we can dismantle the pentad of ethnoracial oppression and remain vigilant against its reemergence in new forms. The establishment of a new mode of temporality should not, therefore, be understood as a finite project leading to a utopian moment of conclusion. Rather, it is a temporal project precisely because it is urgent, perpetual, always at risk of loss, retrogression, and even failure, but is still taken up willfully.

Index